Through the Window
& BEYOND

New Designs for Cathedral Window

Lynne Edwards

Dedication

To
The ever-supportive Brian
Dickon and Tom
Mum and Dad
This book is also dedicated to several
groups of people:
To those who have been kind enough not only to
admire my work but also to actually buy it;
To those who have taken my classes in Cathedral
Window and have not gone home in tears;
To those who have produced their own exciting
work in this area (for which of course
I take full credit);
To those who have been heard to say 'I don't
usually like Cathedral Window, but . . .'

Heartfelt thanks,
Lynne

Acknowledgments

My thanks to the following individuals:
Anne Roberts and Angela Chisholm for providing
extra background information;
Teressa Gordon-Jones, Hazel Hurst, Wendy
Rulton, Chris Swaine, Rosemary Wilkinson, and
Zena Williams for allowing the quilts that they
own to appear in these pages;
Maureen Baker, Audrey Benson, Hilda Bradbury,
Jean Constantine, Edna Farrow, Jo Jeffries,
Elizabeth Snodgrass, Shirley Stocks, and Chris
Wase for their contributions to the Gallery section;
Sara Impey and Ann Larkin for contributing their
inspiring work and ideas;
The Wizard Word Processor and Quilter,
Jean Constantine.

Credits

Editor-in-Chief/Technical Editor **Barbara Weiland**
Managing Editor **Greg Sharp**
Copy Editor **Liz McGehee**
Proofreader **Leslie Phillips**
Illustrators **Brian Metz/Lynne Edwards**
Photographer **Brent Kane**
Design Director **Judy Petry**
Text and Cover Designer **Amy Shayne**
Design Assistant **Claudia L'Heureux**

Through the Window and Beyond
New Designs for Cathedral Window
© 1995 by Lynne Edwards
That Patchwork Place, Inc.
PO Box 118
Bothell, WA 98041-0118 USA

Printed in Hong Kong
00 99 98 97 96 95   6 5 4 3 2 1

Library of Congress Cataloging-in-Publication Data
Edwards, Lynne,
Through the window and beyond : new designs for cathedral
window / by Lynne Edwards.
    p. cm.
ISBN 1-56477-100-8
1. Patchwork—Patterns. 2. Quilting—Patterns. I. Title.
TT835.E378 1995
746.46—dc20   95-6167
                                                                   CIP

Table of Contents

Introducing the Cathedral Window

Cathedral Window is a traditional patchwork technique, usually interpreted in old quilts as rows of folded squares of cream muslin with a random arrangement of patterned fabric squares in the windows. It requires about four times its area in the folded squares, so is very greedy of fabric. The resulting piece of work is also extremely heavy.

When I first learned about the Cathedral Window, I felt that its origins were possibly Victorian, as the fussiness and wastefulness of fabric seemed typical of this era, in England at least. The first documented evidence of this design used in a quilt or bed covering, however, appeared at the Chicago World's Fair of 1933. This seemed to me very surprising, and when discussing it with a couple of fellow enthusiasts from Florida, they reckoned that Cathedral Window could well have flourished in the Depression years when all a quilter had was a pile of plain corn sacks and a few scraps of coloured fabric.

This was a very intriguing theory, but left the history of this popular pattern still shrouded in mystery. Quite recently, more background information has come to light from a completely different direction. Anne Roberts, of Sussex, England, sent me a modern baby carrier that she had bought in China. It was made using the Cathedral Window design. She also sent information from a book on Chinese costume that showed the pattern. Cathedral Window seems to have been used traditionally as a motif mainly on baby carriers and children's clothing. Known as the "coin" pattern, it was a symbol of prosperity and could also be used to ward off evil. How long the design has been around in this way I don't yet know, but I continue to research it.

Angela Chisholm, of Edinburgh, Scotland, has sent me extracts from the catalogue that accompanied a 1990 Exhibition of Korean Wrapping Cloths. These are decorative cloths called *potaji* that are used for wrapping, carrying, or covering a wide variety of objects. They are usually square and are in many sizes. They have been popular since the fifteenth century and include patchwork and the particular technique called *ciatamani*. This is what we now know as Cathedral Window. The photograph in the catalogue shows a detail of one of these cloths. I could see that the method of stitching back the curve is the same one that I use—the spaced backstitch. With these two examples of a long tradition of the technique in the East, I wonder whether returning missionaries could have brought it back to the United States or to England early in this century.

My own interest in Cathedral Window began more than twenty years ago when an inspirational embroideress named Anna Wilson showed it to me. Although already in her seventies, she was a very adventurous and creative textile artist. She showed me how to fold and stitch the Cathedral Window unit, but she never said that it was always done in cream muslin and with scraps. So, my first sample was in gray with black and white windows. She also never said it was difficult so I became hooked, and for the past two decades, I have seldom been without a piece of Cathedral Window as work in progress.

I am totally addicted to Cathedral Window and I have a certain missionary zeal to convert others to see the design potential for colour, shape, and movement in this technique. I teach a wide range of patchwork techniques, both hand and machine, and sometimes I will meet someone I've not seen for awhile and they will ask, "Are you still doing all that Cathedral Window?" I have to reply that yes, I am, and no, I'm not getting tired of it, as there's still so much to explore and develop. I hope that some of you will come to share my obsession with this wonderful design as you try my techniques and come up with your own variations.

In this book, you will learn how to make the classic Cathedral Window and a lovely variation called The Secret Garden. With these two units, a whole new world of designs emerges.

(Facing page) An example of the traditional interpretation of Cathedral Window done in muslin and scraps, 12" x 12", maker and date unknown. Donated by Susan Harvey, Leicestershire, England.

Getting

Started

Any good builder knows that choosing the right materials and assembling the necessary tools are important preliminary steps to creating a masterpiece. The same is true when assembling Cathedral Window units for a quilt project. Making the units does not require much in the way of the special equipment that is so essential to contemporary patchwork methods, such as rotary cutting and speed piecing. Basically, you need good fabric, a basic sewing kit, and a steam iron. I prepare for a lovely, long hand-sewing session by folding and pressing (or machine stitching and pressing) six or eight background squares that I store in a rigid plastic box with my sewing kit. Then I'm ready to stitch away wherever I happen to be.

Perhaps one of the reasons for my commitment to Cathedral Window in the past was the lack of any workroom space or area where I could machine sew easily without having to clear everything away for the next meal. Chauffeuring and attending to small boys means that either you do portable handwork or you don't do anything. Now that our boys are grown up and one has left home, I have gained a workroom so I tend to move from hand to machine work as the mood strikes me.

Machine stitching, I find, is a daytime activity for me when I'm fresh. Handwork soothes and relaxes me after a day's teaching. Until they make a sewing machine that says "Put your feet up, dear, and just relax," there will always be a place for hand-sewn patchwork in my repertoire.

Selecting Fabric

Cathedral Window units can be made from a much wider choice of fabrics than you would use for many other traditional patchwork techniques. To get an idea of the possibilities, examine the photos of the quilts in this book. You will see that the quiltmakers have taken this design to new vistas through the use of a variety of fabrics. You will need to choose fabric for the background squares and for the "windows."

The "windows" can be made of virtually any fabric you wish to use. Stabilize flimsy or soft fabrics by backing them with a fusible (iron-on) interfacing before cutting out the windows. You can treat silky

fabrics that fray badly in the same way to prevent the edges from raveling away while you work. The windows need not be made of a single fabric. Consider piecing some miniature crazy patchwork for the window, for example.

The window is placed on top of folded squares of the chosen background fabric, so you don't have to worry about the weights being equal or the fabrics being of the same type. Consider using silk, jersey, or any kind of glitzy fabric as well as cottons. Thick velvets can be hard to handle with this technique, but if you don't mind struggling a bit, go for it.

The background folded squares must take a good press, so avoid crease-resistant poly/cotton blends. Test also in case you have a fabric that, when pressed with a steam iron, will shrink in one direction but not the other. Using a fabric that shrinks in one dimension will most definitely end in tears and frustration. If the fabric you want to use is floppy or lightweight, consider spraying it with spray starch and pressing it before cutting out the squares. Spray starch firms up the fabric beautifully, making it easier to cut and prepare for stitching. Once you begin to stitch, the fabric softens again.

Don't be afraid to embellish the windows. Use beads or decorative thread if you want to add surface texture.

Cutting and Sewing Equipment

Most of us quilters use a rotary cutter, ruler, and mat for cutting squares as it speeds up the process and increases accuracy. I always cut the squares for Cathedral Window in this way, cutting several layers at once. The templates for rectangular Cathedral Windows are such irregular shapes, however, that I have to draw 'round them with a sharp pencil and then cut with good scissors. The same applies to the windows: I cut the squares with a ruler and rotary cutter, but for odd shapes, I draw 'round the templates and cut them out by hand.

Listed on page 8 are the general sewing supplies you will need to make Cathedral Windows. As noted earlier, I keep the small items handy along with several prepared background squares so I can carry them along and do handwork at odd moments when my hands are free.

Needle and Thread. I like to use 100% cotton thread and Sharp needles. If the fabric is soft, I can use a Sharp #12, but if it is a firm polished-cotton fabric, I find the finer needle bends too easily and I have to use a Sharp #10. It is important to match the colour of the thread as nearly as possible to the background folded squares. A shade darker is better than lighter. The best test is to lay a thread across the fabric to see if it visually disappears. Sometimes I find I have to use a polyester thread because that is the only way I can get a good colour match.

Pins. I use dressmakers' long, extra-fine pins, as they are fine enough to pin through all the folded layers without difficulty but they do not bend. Glass-headed pins drive me mad as I keep getting the thread wound 'round the heads as I stitch. But they may be your absolute favourite, so do use whatever you find most comfortable and efficient.

Sewing Machine. When making Cathedral Window squares, I seldom use the sewing machine, but always use it for constructing the rectangles. Try both ways of making the folded squares and choose for yourself whichever you like best. I don't believe that one method is better than the other. We just need to do what pleases us best and what works best for the job in hand.

A basic straight stitch with an accurate 1/4"-wide seam allowance is all that is required, so even an ancient hand machine would do. Remember to use a new size 80/11 needle for medium-weight cotton fabrics. Choose a needle of the appropriate weight for other heavier or lighter-weight fabrics.

Steam Iron. Good, firm pressing is essential for Cathedral Window, whether the first stage is machine stitched or not. A steam iron is ideal, but a spray bottle of water can be used alongside a dry iron as an alternative.

Templates. When making a template from those printed in this book, trace the desired shape onto thick tracing paper or graph paper. Cut out around the shape about 1/4" beyond the edge of the template and glue it to an index card or a manila folder. Then cut out the template shape itself, cutting on the inside edge of the drawn line so that the template remains accurate. Cutting outside the drawn line may result in an inaccurate template that is larger than desired. If you prefer, you can trace templates onto template plastic, then cut them from the plastic.

Marking Pencils. Use marking pencils that will give a fine, accurate line. Silver or white pencils are good for marking dark fabrics; a well-sharpened lead pencil shows best on light-coloured fabrics.

Making

Classic

Cathedral

Windows

The classic Cathedral Window unit requires two folded squares of background fabric plus one smaller square for the window. There are two methods for constructing the folded square. One is by hand using a steam iron and the other is by machine. All stitching should be as inconspicuous as possible.

Cutting the Squares

1. Determine the size of the square to be cut by multiplying the desired finished measurement by 2 and then adding ½" to allow for ¼"-wide seam allowances all around. For example, if you want 3" finished squares, cut 6½" background squares. Refer to the illustration below for other cutting and finished sizes.

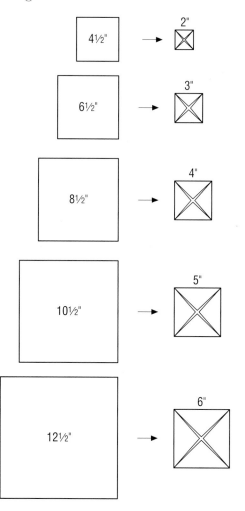

2. Cut two squares of fabric of the chosen size by drawing around a template of the correct size or by using a rotary cutter, ruler, and mat.

Preparing the Squares by Hand

This is my favourite method of construction because it gives beautifully flat and balanced corners to each window. It is more time-consuming than the machine-stitched method and a little less durable, but I am happy to pay that price for the effect once it's finished. The folded and pressed piece is called an "envelope" in the directions below—because it looks like one.

1. Using the point of the iron, fix the center of each large square by folding diagonally and pressing lightly, first one way and then the other. It is not necessary to press a crease along the entire fold, just at the center.

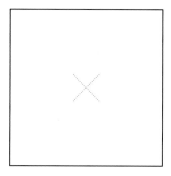

Crease the center diagonals.

2. Unfold each square and with the wrong side of the fabric uppermost, turn in each edge ¼" and press firmly. Don't bother with basting or pinning. If you are used to working with ¼"-wide seam allowances, you should be able to "eye" this rather than taking the time to measure. Run the point of the steam iron along each edge as you fold it.

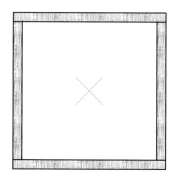

3. Fold each corner, one by one, to the center of the square, where they should meet. Each outside corner should have a nice sharp point. Press.

Tip

If you are lucky, the folding and pressing procedure described above will work out just as stated. However, this is often the stage where things start to look wrong and where the beginner's confidence disappears. If this is the case:

1. Press the square back to its original flat shape with the ¹/₄" allowances pressed in place and begin again. First take one corner to the center and press lightly. Now take the next corner to the center. If they fail to meet and one seems much longer than the other, as shown, adjust them so that they are even with each other at the center.

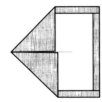

This usually results in a blunt corner at the outside point.

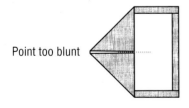

Point too blunt

2. To remedy this, pull the two center corners across the middle until the outside corner is really sharp. If this means that the center corners do not lie exactly on the marked midpoint (or even overlap), don't worry. The important thing is to get the outside corners very sharp and to press well.

Mid-points overlap slightly.

4. If the center points are not lying in a cross shape, readjust until they are, even if this means that the envelope no longer lies flat. Secure the center points by sewing two tiny stitches through all layers, starting and finishing at the back, where the thread can be left ready for the next step. Keep the stitches very small so that they are barely noticeable and bury all knots so they do not show.

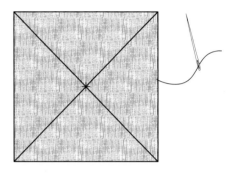

5. Using the steam iron, press again on each of the four outer corners. Do not press the whole envelope, as it may be uneven and you will not be able to press it flat.

6. Bring the four corners to the center again and press, still keeping them as sharp as possible. Any nasty puffy bits within the shape will be lost in the folded area as the points are brought to the middle. Using the original thread, sew the center down firmly through all layers. Again, the stitches should form a tiny cross. I usually repeat the pair of stitches and pull them very firmly to keep those four corners tightly held in the center. End by burying a knot as you do when hand quilting. The four outside corners can be made sharper if necessary by pinching them into shape and pressing.

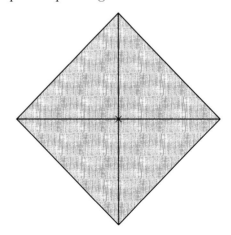

Preparing the Squares by Machine

This method eliminates the first stages of folding and pressing. Instead, you use the sewing machine to stitch the square into its envelope shape. It is quicker and more secure than the hand method described above. The chief drawback is the bulkiness that results at the corners, but there are some strategies to reduce this.

1. Fold each square of fabric in half with right sides together. Pin. Stitch ¼" from each end.

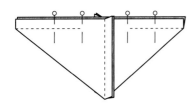

Wrong side

Fold

2. Pull the open edges of the folded and stitched unit apart and refold, with seam lines matching. Pin, then stitch from each corner to within 1" of the seam at the center.

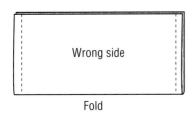

3. To reduce the bulk, trim the corners and then press the seams open. Use the point of the iron and try not to press a crease in the outer edges of the folded shape.

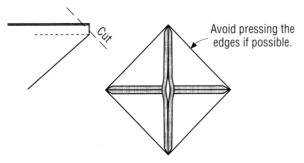

Cut

Avoid pressing the edges if possible.

4. Turn the folded square right side out through the center opening and press. The square is now at the first fold stage shown in step 3 on page 11.

5. To close the opening in the center, draw the two edges together and take two tiny stitches at the center through all layers. Begin and end the stitching on the back. Leave the thread and needle in place, ready for the next stage.

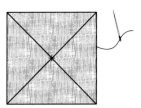

6. Bring each corner to the center in turn, pressing firmly and keeping the outside corners as sharp as possible. Using the original thread, sew the center down firmly through all layers. Fasten off at the back of the work. Again, the stitches should form a tiny cross. I usually repeat the pair of stitches and pull them very firmly to keep those four corners tightly held in the center. The finished unit will look like the one shown above; it will just be smaller.

Joining the Squares

After folding two background squares, you are ready to join them. To do so, place them right sides together (the sides with the envelope appearance) and join with hand whipstitching. To avoid knots that show, begin with small backstitches in the folded edge of the squares.

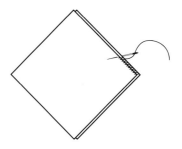

Adding the Windows

The size of the window square varies with the size of the folded squares. The diagram below gives window templates for the most frequently used sizes. Make templates or use the dimensions given in the chart to rotary cut the squares.

If you have chosen a size not shown here, just measure from the center to one corner of the folded square and cut a square approximately the same size as this. It will be a little too large, but can be trimmed down later.

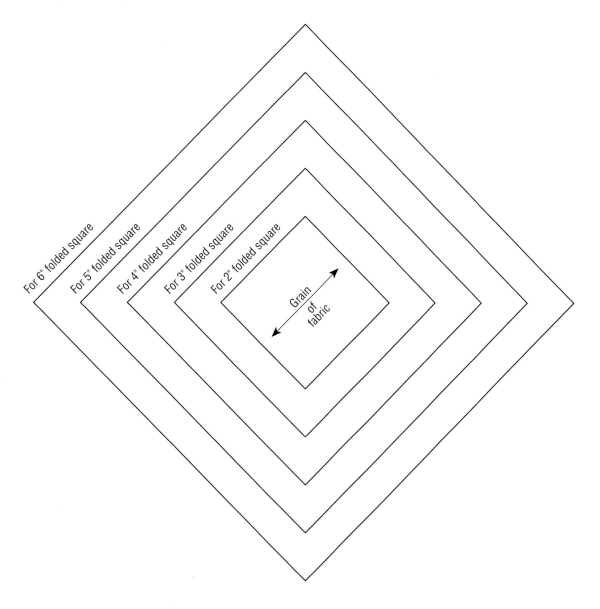

To add a window:

1. Lay the square of window fabric over the center square that formed across the joined envelope shapes. Trim it down if necessary until approximately ⅛" of the background fabric shows all around. Pin in position, keeping the pins in the center of the work as shown.

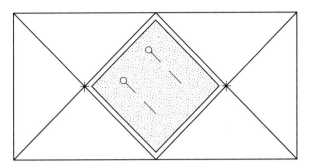

2. Beginning in one corner, roll the surrounding border over the edge of the window square, stretching the bias edge to create a curve and stitching it down onto the square. Don't be afraid to really stretch that edge so that the curve is as much as ¼" at its widest point. This makes that lovely circular shape that links several blocks when joined together. Stitch the rolled edge down, using either an invisible hemming stitch or tiny, spaced backstitches placed close to the folded edge. See illustration following step 3.

3. Since all raw edges of the window must be covered, stop stitching at least ¼" from the corner and bring both bias edges over the window. Secure them with a double bartack stitch, stitching through all layers to give the corner more strength.

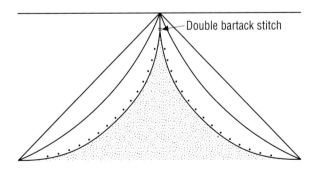
Double bartack stitch

You will find that the corners do not look identical. Those over the seam joining the blocks together will be very smooth and sharp. The other two corners will not look like this, especially if the squares were prepared by hand rather than by machine. (See page 10.) These corners will appear more wedge shaped as shown below.

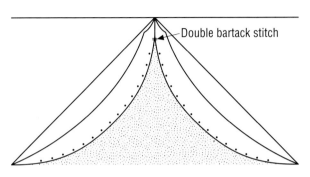
Double bartack stitch

Don't worry—you haven't done anything wrong. Just adjust each side so it appears balanced in shape and make the double bartack stitch as usual. If you have machine stitched the squares, the corners will tend to be a bit bulky and will not lie quite as flat as the other two. Again, try to make both sides as equal and balanced as possible.

4. Sew around all four sides, finishing with the final bartack stitches. This is the basic Cathedral Window process. As you add folded squares to this unit, add windows in the same manner described here.

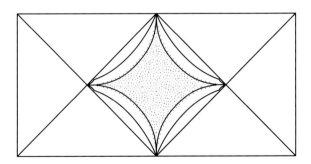

Adding Corner and Edge Treatments

In the three classic Cathedral Window projects that begin on page 16, the corner and edge sections around the windows are left unturned. This gives a straight-edged frame to the design.

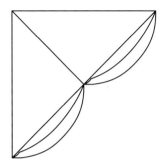

You may turn back the corners and edges as Cathedral Window curves without adding any extra fabric for a partial window.

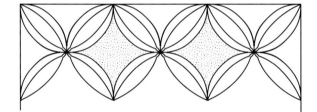

If you decide to use this treatment, take care when turning corners back to keep the outer edge of the block and the corner in shape.

You can extend the window to the outer edges by trimming the window squares as shown below and laying them in position on the triangular shapes at the edges of the block.

Trimmed square of
window fabric for
edges and corners

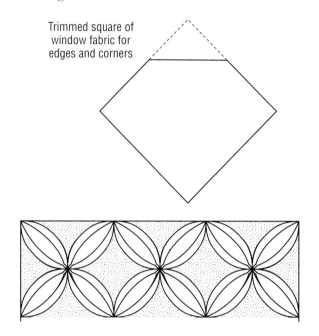

Fold the extending edges of the window fabric over the edge of the block and stitch them down on the back as shown.

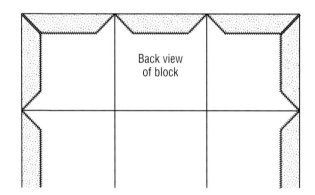

Back view
of block

Then secure the half-windows as you would for complete windows.

Cathedral Window Projects

Now that you know the basic steps for creating the Cathedral Window unit, it's time to try your hand at stitching Cathedral Window projects. If you have never tried this technique before, begin with a small project made of nine background squares. Then graduate to the "Knot Garden Quilt" or the "Cathedral Window Cushion." Before you begin a project, it would be a good idea to read "Finishing Techniques for Cathedral Window Quilts," which begins on page 96. They require special techniques that differ from traditional quiltmaking methods.

Three Sample Blocks *by Lynne Edwards, 1994, Suffolk, England. Each block measures 11" x 11". Each shows a different arrangement of windows on the same nine folded squares.*

Cathedral Window Cushion *by Lynne Edwards, 1994, Suffolk, England, 19" x 19". This simple design was executed using two background fabrics with windows of lawn and silk noil.*

Knot Garden Quilt *by Lynne Edwards, 1982, Suffolk, England, 75" x 93". The formal Tudor Knot Gardens inspired this quilt, made of twenty Cathedral Window blocks in many shades of green. Owned by Hazel Hurst.*

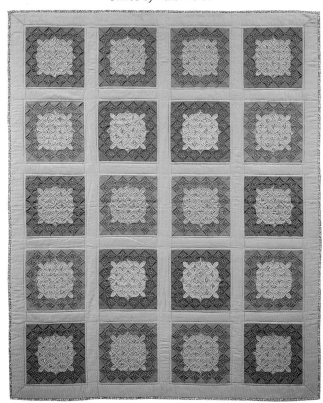

NINE-SQUARE BLOCK

Colour photo on page 16

Finished Block Size: 12" x 12"

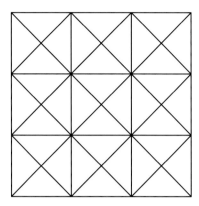

Block Plan

Materials

9 squares, each 8½" x 8½", for folded
background squares

Scraps of 2 different fabrics for windows,
each approximately 9" x 9"

Construction

1. Using the 8½" background squares, construct 9 folded squares, using your choice of the hand or machine methods shown on pages 10–12. When completed, they will be 4" folded squares.
2. Whipstitch the folded squares together to make 3 rows of 3 squares each.

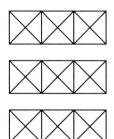

Window Plans

3. Whipstitch the rows together, matching seams carefully to complete the Nine-Square block as shown above.
4. If you prefer to cut with templates, make a template for a 4" window, tracing the appropriate square on page 13. Using the template (or rotary-cutting methods if you prefer), cut a total of 12 windows from the two window fabrics.
5. Position the windows on the Nine-Square block in the desired design. See layouts above.
6. Working from the center out, stitch each window in place, matching the sewing thread to the background folded fabric. Follow the directions for "Adding the Windows" on pages 13–14.

CATHEDRAL WINDOW CUSHION

Colour photo on page 16
Finished Cushion Size: 19" x 19"

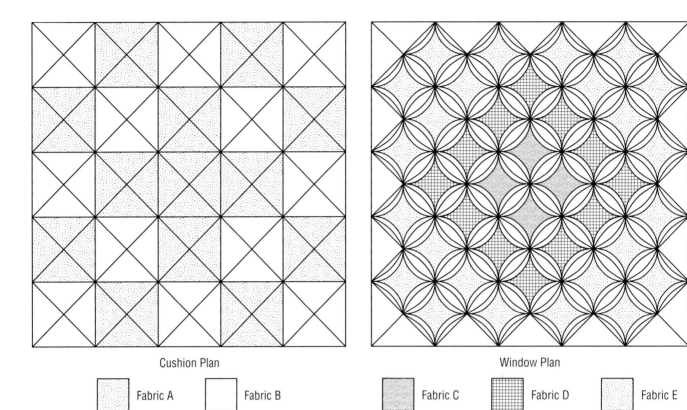

Cushion Plan

☐ Fabric A   ☐ Fabric B

Window Plan

☐ Fabric C   ☐ Fabric D   ☐ Fabric E

This cushion requires two different fabrics for the background folded squares and three different fabrics for the windows.

Materials

(44"-wide fabric)
⅝ yd. Fabric A for background squares
½ yd. Fabric B for background squares
⅛ yd. each of 3 different fabrics (Fabrics C, D, and E) for windows
⅝ yd. fabric for borders and cushion back
24" x 24" square of lightweight muslin
polyester fiberfill for stuffing or a foam cushion

Cutting and Construction

1. Cut 13 squares, each 6½" x 6½", from Fabric A and 12 squares, each 6½" x 6½", from Fabric B.
2. Using the 6½" background squares, construct 25 folded squares, using your choice of the hand or machine methods that begin on page 10. When completed, they will be 3" folded squares.
3. Arrange the squares as shown above left.
4. Whipstitch the folded squares together to make 5 rows of 5 squares each. Whipstitch the rows together to complete the five-by-five background for the window. Match seams carefully.
5. If you prefer to cut with templates, make a win-

dow template for a 3" folded square, tracing the appropriate square on page 13.

6. Using the template (or rotary-cutting methods if you prefer), cut 4 windows from Fabric C, 12 windows from Fabric D, and 24 windows from Fabric E, for a total of 40 windows.

7. Working from the center out and referring to the directions for "Adding the Windows" on page 13, pin and stitch each window in place as shown in the window plan on page 18.

8. Cut 2½"-wide strips from the border fabric, referring to "Adding Sashing and Borders" on page 97 for measuring and cutting directions. Sew the borders to the cushion top as shown, mitering the corners.

Finishing

1. Place the completed cushion front face up on top of the muslin square, trim the muslin to match, and baste the two layers together.

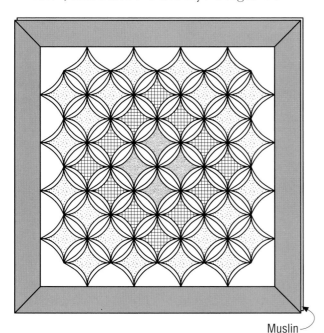

Muslin

2. Cut the backing to match the cushion cover size. With right sides facing, sew the layers together, using a ¼"-wide seam allowance and leaving an opening on one edge.

3. Turn the cushion cover right side out and add the pillow form or stuff with fiberfill. Whipstitch the opening edges together.

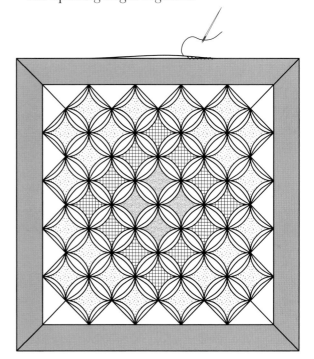

KNOT GARDEN QUILT

Colour photo on page 16

Finished Quilt Size: 75" x 93" Finished Block Size: 15" x 15"

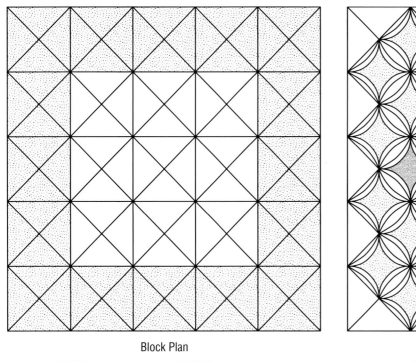

Block Plan

☐ Light Fabrics   ▨ Dark Fabrics

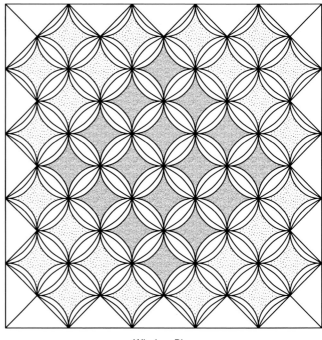

Window Plan

▨ Fabric A   ▨ Fabric B

This quilt is made of twenty Cathedral Window blocks. Each block begins with a combination of nine light-coloured folded squares in the center, surrounded by dark-coloured squares. The lights and darks vary from block to block.

Two patterned (Liberty of London™ Tana™ Lawn) fabrics (Fabric A and Fabric B) were used for the windows in each block and arranged as shown above right.

Materials

(44"-wide fabric)

6 yds. total assorted light fabrics for folded background squares*

10 yds. total assorted dark fabrics for folded background squares*

1 yd. Fabric A for center windows

1½ yds. Fabric B for outer windows

2½ yds. for sashing

2½ yds. of 2-ounce batting

5¼ yds. for backing

⅜ yd. for binding

* If you prefer, you can use only one light and one dark fabric, but introducing several similar shades adds interest and depth to the quilt.

Cutting and Block Construction

For each of the 20 blocks required:

1. Cut 9 squares, each 6½" x 6½", from a light-coloured fabric, and 16 squares, each 6½" x 6½", from a dark-coloured fabric.

2. Using the 6½" background squares, construct 9 light background squares and 16 dark background squares, using your choice of the hand or machine methods that begin on page 10. When completed, they will be 3" folded squares.

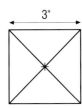

3. Arrange the squares, following the layout in the block illustration on page 20.

4. Whipstitch the folded squares together in rows of 5 squares each, then whipstitch the rows together to form the block, matching the seams carefully.

Tip

If you prefer to work on smaller pieces, join 3 rows of blocks and 2 rows of blocks. Then add as many windows (steps 5, 6, and 7 below) as you can before sewing the two sections together and adding the remaining windows.

5. If you prefer to use templates for cutting, make a window template for a 3" folded square by tracing the appropriate square on page 13. You may rotary cut the window squares if you wish.

6. From Fabric A for the central windows, cut 16 windows. From Fabric B for the outer windows, cut 24 windows.

7. Working from the center of the block out, pin and stitch each window in position, referring to the directions for "Adding the Windows" on page 13 and the window plan on page 20.

Quilt Top Assembly

1. From the sashing fabric, cut the following strips along the length of the fabric. Be careful not to include selvages in any of the strips. (Shaded key indicates placement location in the quilt, *not* color. See page 22.)

  Strip A: 15 strips, each 3½" x 15½", for vertical sashing

  Strip B: 4 strips, each 3½" x 69½", for horizontal sashing

  Strip C: 2 strips, each 3½" x 87½", for outer side sashing

  Strip D: 2 strips, each 3½" x 75½", for outer top and bottom sashing

2. Cut a matching strip of batting for each sashing strip. Pair each vertical sashing strip A with a matching strip of batting, placing the sashing strip right side up on the batting strip. Machine stitch ¼" from the raw edges.

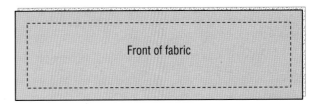

Front of fabric

3. Trim away the batting close to the stitching lines.

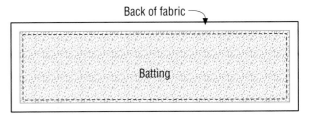

Back of fabric

Batting

4. Turn the ¼"-wide seam allowance to the batting side of each strip, with the machine stitching right along the fold. Miter the corners. Repeat with the remaining sashing strips.

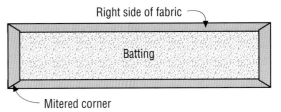

Right side of fabric

Batting

Mitered corner

5. Arrange the completed Cathedral Window blocks in 5 rows of 4 blocks each with short sashing strips between them.

6. With right sides facing, whipstitch the blocks and short sashing strips together in rows.

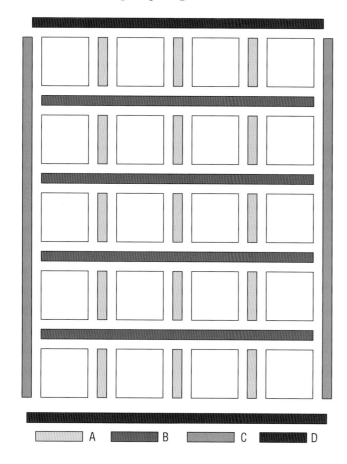

7. Prepare the horizontal sashing strips B in the same manner as the short vertical sashing strips.

(See steps 2–4 on page 21.) Whipstitch the completed rows of blocks together with sashing strips B between them.

8. Prepare the side sashing strips C and the top and bottom sashing strips D as you did the other sashing strips, but leave one long edge on each unstitched.

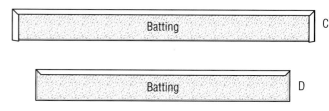

9. Whipstitch the side strips to the quilt and then add the top and bottom strips in the same manner to complete the quilt top.

Finishing

For each of the following steps, refer to "Finishing Techniques for Cathedral Window Quilts," beginning on page 96.

1. Prepare the backing.
2. Smooth the completed quilt top in place on top of the wrong side of the backing.
3. Tie the Cathedral Window blocks at regular intervals to hold the heavy blocks in place on the backing.
4. Quilt ¼" away from the seams in the sashing or add a more elaborate quilting design if desired.
5. Bind the edges.

The

Secret

Garden

Variation

This easy variation of the classic Cathedral Window creates a pretty four-pointed flower.

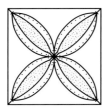

While the traditional Cathedral Window requires at least two folded background squares before you can add a window, with this variation you can create individual units because each one requires only one folded square and a contrasting window. You may use any size square. Cut the windows the same size as the finished folded background square. For example, a background square that has a cut size of 8½" x 8½" finishes to 4" x 4" when folded. For the window in this square, you would cut a 4" square of contrasting fabric.

Whipstitch the finished Secret Garden units together as shown for the classic Cathedral Window on page 12 to create the quilt top of the size, shape, and design you desire.

Making Secret Garden Units

1. Prepare the background squares as shown for the classic Cathedral Window, using your choice of the hand or machine methods that begin on page 10. After bringing the 4 final corners to the center, press them well but do not stitch them down. After pressing them in place, unfold. The fold lines should be clearly visible.

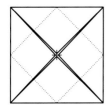

Dotted lines are
pressed crease lines.

2. Cut a square of contrasting fabric for the window, cutting it the same size as the finished folded background square.

3. Lay the square of window fabric in position on top of the background square, using the fold lines as a guide for positioning. Trim the window square slightly so that the fold lines are just visible beyond it. Sew the square in place, using a small running stitch ⅛" from the edge through all layers.

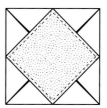

4. Bring the four outside corners of the background square to the center over the window square and press. Refer to the Tip on page 11 for the classic Cathedral Window to achieve sharp corners and stitch down firmly.

5. Insert a pin about ¼" from each corner through all layers.

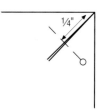

6. Working from the center out, turn the edges of the background square back, ending at the pin. Stitch in place with tiny, evenly spaced backstitches, and when you reach the pin, remove it and secure with 2 bartack stitches across the bias edges of the background square, making sure the stitches go through all layers. Repeat this in each corner. You may also bartack the center as shown for the classic Cathedral Window if desired.

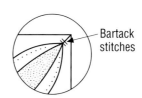 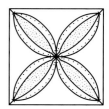

Bartack
stitches

Creating Secret Garden Designs

You can use just two fabrics, and by reversing the placement in alternate blocks, you can create a chequerboard effect.

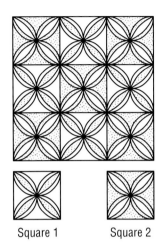

Square 1   Square 2

If you sew two strips of fabric together to make the window squares, the colours create an interlocking design when the blocks are joined as shown in the illustrations below and above right.

When you create a chequerboard window square, the design has a diagonal emphasis.

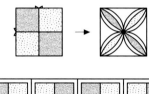

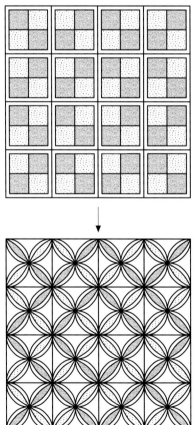

Designing with Cathedral Window and Secret Garden Units

Cathedral Window designs require several folded squares to create the resulting pattern of diamond windows. It takes only one Secret Garden window for a resulting design element. This essential difference can be used to create many exciting effects in design and colour.

Secret Garden Frame

Use Secret Garden units to create a frame for a central panel of Cathedral Window units as shown here in "Blue Hanging."

The squares marked "A" in the illustration at right are slightly different than the others. They appear to be Secret Garden units, but the inner window fabric has been left out so that one side of the square could be used as part of the central Cathedral Window design. Refer to the photo of "Blue Hanging."

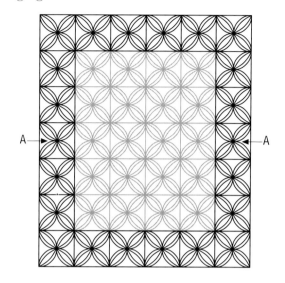

Secret Garden Corners

Using a block with a classic Cathedral Window unit at the center and Secret Garden units in the

Blue Hanging *by Lynne Edwards, 1987, Suffolk, England, 25¼" x 28". The design for this small hanging features Cathedral Window and Secret Garden units with windows of vibrantly colored silks.*

Starry Windows *Block by Lynne Edwards, 1993, Suffolk, England, 11" x 11". This Ninepatch design combines Cathedral Window and Secret Garden units in vivid shades of blue and green.*

corner-square positions creates a simple, yet effective design. See "Starry Windows" on page 26.

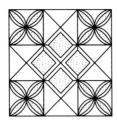

Using the same principle in a four-by-four block configuration creates a design with more impact in the center as seen in "Silver Salmon" below.

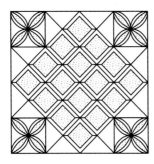

The design for the "Purple Quilt" at right was sparked by the striped cotton fabric used in the center squares of each block. Using three Secret Garden squares in each corner created a background for the stepped Cathedral Window center. Although I didn't consciously intend it, the quilt finished up with a very rich ecclesiastical look to it. Step-by-step directions for making this quilt begin on page 30.

Following the same quilt plan, I made the "Aldeburgh Quilt," shown on page 28, for Mr. and Mrs. Schaafsma from the Netherlands, old friends of my parents. For the windows, I used silk and printed lawn, and for the background squares, ten different shades of green polished cotton fabrics. The sashing in two shades of silk meets printed lawn cornerstones. Note how different this quilt looks because of the colours chosen.

Purple Quilt *by Lynne Edwards, 1985, Suffolk, England, 53" x 87". Rich shades of mauve and a multicoloured striped fabric were used to create this design with ecclesiastical overtones.*

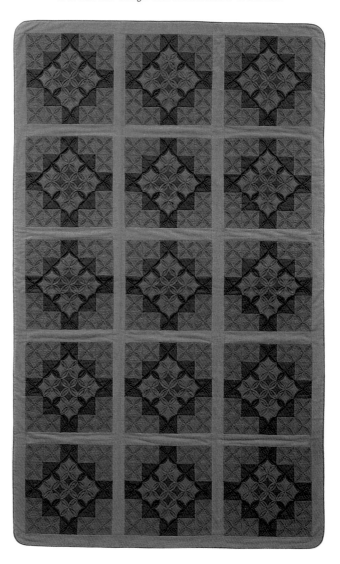

Silver Salmon *block by Lynne Edwards, 1993, Suffolk, England, 11½" x 11½". Two exotic furnishing (home-decorator) fabrics were used for the folded squares, and several shades of silk were used for the windows.*

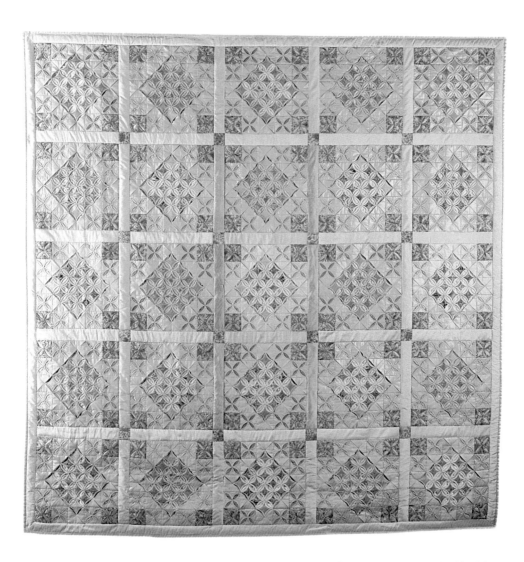

Aldeburgh Quilt *by Lynne Edwards, 1991, Suffolk, England, 87" x 87". The twenty-five blocks in this shimmery quilt were made using the same type of folded squares as in the Purple Quilt, but the results are completely different due to the color use and placement. Owned by Mr. and Mrs. Schaafsma, Holland. Photograph by Bruce Head.*

Secret Garden Centers

A very different and often surprising effect appears when a central area of Secret Garden folded squares is surrounded by a border of classic Cathedral Window as shown in the "Indigo Block" shown on page 29.

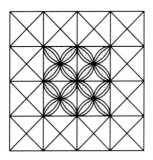

Using patterned fabric for the Secret Garden folded squares in the "Peacock Windows" wall hanging created a very strong center. It appears to be done in a larger scale than the surrounding Cathedral Window units, but in reality, they are all the same size. The central area of Secret Garden units was made from squares of textured and hand-dyed fabrics surrounded by Cathedral Window units. The luminous quality of the windows was achieved by using silk, both in the Cathedral Window and in the more hidden Secret Garden windows. These have a diamond-shaped emphasis, created by using pieced chequerboard squares (page 25) for the Secret Garden windows. Complete directions for this quilt begin on page 32.

Indigo Block *by Lynne Edwards, 1993, Suffolk, England, 12 1/2" x 12 1/2". African fabrics were used for this block, which has a strong center of Secret Garden units framed by classic Cathedral Window squares.*

In the "Silver Blue Tower" wall hanging, classic Cathedral Window units form the central tower, with Secret Garden units for the sky. The folded squares for the tower were arranged in individual squares so that the colour flows from dark at the base upwards to the lighter shades. The windows complement this by also shading from dark to light upwards.

Background squares of gray silk in the Secret Garden sky have only two petal shapes instead of four to create the diagonal effect that makes the area less dominant than the tower. The fabrics used in the Secret Garden windows gradate diagonally from the palest in the bottom right corner to darkest in the top left corner. The occasional use of striped fabrics in the tower, both as folded squares and as windows, adds an interesting effect. Complete directions for this quilt begin on page 34.

Silver Blue Tower *by Lynne Edwards, 1988, Suffolk, England, 24" x 31 1/2". The Cathedral Window tower of delicately coloured silks sits amidst a background of Secret Garden squares.*

Peacock Windows *by Lynne Edwards, 1994, Suffolk, England, 38" x 38". Blue and green silk windows glow on a background of squares made of hand-dyed fabric.*

PURPLE QUILT

Colour photo on page 27

Finished Quilt Size: 53" x 87"   Finished Block Size: 15" x 15"

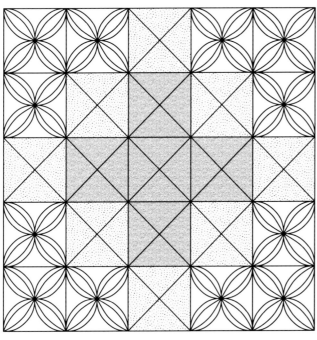

Block Plan

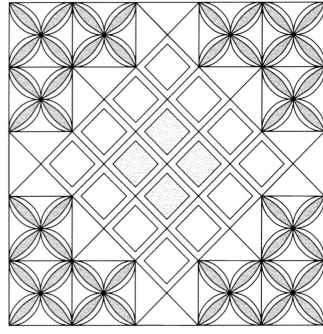

Window Plan

 Fabric A   Fabric B   ☐ Fabric C

Materials

(44"-wide fabric)
4 yds. Fabric A
4 yds. Fabric B
6½ yds. Fabric C
2½ yds. fabric for sashing and borders
5 yds. for backing
2½ yds. of 2-ounce batting
¼ yd. for binding

Cutting and Block Construction

To make the 15 blocks required for this quilt:

1. From Fabric A, cut:
     75 squares, each 6½" x 6½", for Cathedral
      Window units
     180 squares, each 3" x 3", for windows in
      Secret Garden units
    From Fabric B, cut:
     120 squares, each 6½" x 6½", for Cathedral
      Window units
    From Fabric C, cut:
     180 squares, each 6½" x 6½", for Secret
      Garden units

2. Construct each of the folded squares for the Cathedral Window units from Fabric A and Fabric B, following the directions beginning on page 10. Finished squares will measure 3" x 3".

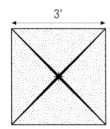

3. Construct 12 Secret Garden squares for each block from Fabric C with windows from Fabric A, following the directions for "Making Secret Garden Units" on page 24. The finished squares will measure 3" x 3".

4. Arrange the squares, following the block plan on page 30. Whipstitch the squares together in rows as shown on page 12, then sew the rows together to form the block, matching seams carefully.

5. Make a window template for a 3" folded square by tracing the appropriate template on page 13. Cut (or rotary cut) 4 windows for each block from Fabric B for the center windows. Cut 12 windows for each block from Fabric C.

6. Working from the center of the block out, pin and stitch each window in position as shown in the window plan on page 30.

Quilt Top Assembly

1. Arrange the blocks in 3 vertical rows of 5 blocks each, leaving 3" of space between the blocks for sashing strips. See illustration above right.

2. From the sashing fabric, cut the following strips, cutting along the length of the fabric.
   - Strip A: 12 strips, each 2½" x 15½", for short horizontal sashing strips between blocks
   - Strip B: 4 strips, each 2½" x 83½", for vertical sashing strips and outer border strips
   - Strip C: 2 strips, each 2½" x 53½", for top and bottom border strips

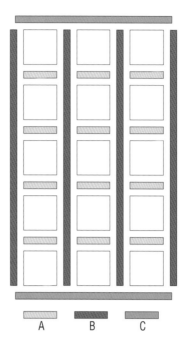

A B C

3. Cut a matching strip of batting for each sashing and border strip. Prepare the sashing strips and assemble the vertical rows with sashing strips in between as shown for the "Knot Garden Quilt" on page 21.

4. Prepare the vertical border strips by stitching the batting to each strip along 3 sides as shown in step 8 on page 98.

5. Prepare the horizontal border strips by stitching ¼" from one long edge only.

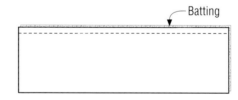

6. Trim the batting close to the machine stitching.

7. Whipstitch the vertical border strips to the long edges of the quilt. Then add the top and bottom borders in the same manner.

Finishing

Refer to "Finishing Techniques for Cathedral Window Quilts," beginning on page 96.

1. Prepare the backing as directed in step 1 on page 99. Pin the quilt to the wrong side of the backing and tie the blocks to the backing at regular intervals to hold the heavy folded squares in position on the backing fabric.

2. Trim and bind the quilt edges.

PEACOCK WINDOWS

Colour photo on page 29
Finished Quilt Size: 38" x 38"

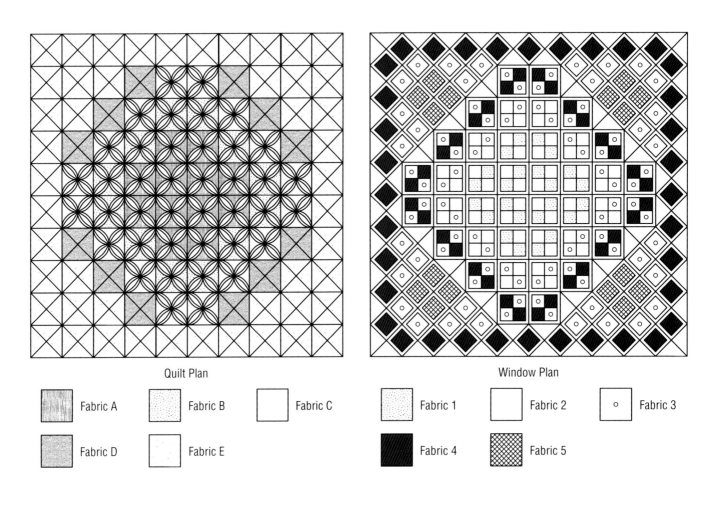

Quilt Plan

Fabric A Fabric B Fabric C

Fabric D Fabric E

Window Plan

Fabric 1 Fabric 2 ∘ Fabric 3

Fabric 4 Fabric 5

Materials

(44"-wide fabric)
½ yd. each of Fabrics A, B, C, and D
1½ yds. Fabric E
½ yd. each of 5 gradated shades of silk
(Window Fabrics #1, #2, #3, #4, #5)
1⅛ yds. for borders
1⅛ yds. of 2-ounce batting
1⅛ yds. for backing
¼ yd. for binding

Cutting and Block Construction

1. Cut the required number of 6½" x 6½" squares from each of the following fabrics.

   Fabric A: 12
   Fabric B: 12
   Fabric C: 16
   Fabric D: 12
   Fabric E: 48

Note

The windows in the Secret Garden units are made of four-patch squares, each 3" x 3". Refer to the illustration above for colour placement as you make the chequerboard windows.

2. For the 12 center windows, cut 1 strip of Fabric #1 and 1 strip of Fabric #2, cutting them each 1¾" x 43". With right sides together, stitch the strips ¼" from one long raw edge. Press the seam toward the darker strip. From the strip-pieced unit, cut 24 segments, each 1¾" wide. Join the segments in pairs as shown. Use these windows for the center units as shown in the illustration above.

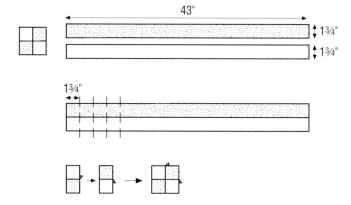

3. For the next set of chequerboard windows, cut 1 strip of Fabric #1 and 1 of Fabric #3. Cut strips 1¾" x 43". Referring to step 2, sew the strips together and press. Then crosscut 24 segments, each 1¾"-wide, from the resulting strip-pieced unit. Sew the segments together in four-patch units as shown.

4. For the next set of windows, cut 1 strip, 1¾" x 43", and 1 strip, 1¾" x 15", from each of Fabrics #3 and #4. Referring to step 2, stitch the long strips together and the short strips together, then press. Crosscut a total of 24 segments from the long strip-pieced unit and 8 from the short unit for a total of 32. Join segments in pairs as shown for a total of 16 chequerboard windows.

5. Construct the Secret Garden units as shown in the directions beginning on page 24. Use the windows of Fabrics #1 and #2 in the Fabric A squares. Use the windows of Fabrics #1 and #3 in the Fabric B squares and use the remaining 16 windows in the Fabric C squares.

6. Construct 12 Cathedral Window background squares from Fabric D and 48 from Fabric E, following the directions beginning on page 10.

Quilt Top Assembly and Finishing

1. Arrange the completed squares, following the quilt plan and window plan on page 32.

2. Join the squares in rows, then stitch the rows together, matching seams carefully.

3. If you prefer to use templates for cutting the windows for the Cathedral Window units that surround the Secret Garden center, make a window template for a 3" folded square by tracing the appropriate square on page 13. You may rotary cut the window squares if you prefer.

4. Following the window plan on page 32, cut 16 windows from Fabric #5, 32 windows from Fabric #3, and 36 windows from Fabric #4.

5. Working from the inner squares out to the corners, pin and stitch each window in position.

6. Following the directions beginning on page 97, measure, cut, back with batting, and add mitered borders to the quilt top. Cut border strips and batting strips 5" wide.

7. Back the quilt and tie at regular intervals to hold the layers together, referring to the directions on page 99.

8. Quilt as desired or mark quilting lines from each seam junction out to the edge of the border, continuing the diagonal line from each folded block.

9. Bind the edges.

SILVER BLUE TOWER

Colour photo on page 29
Finished Quilt Size: 25½" x 34½"

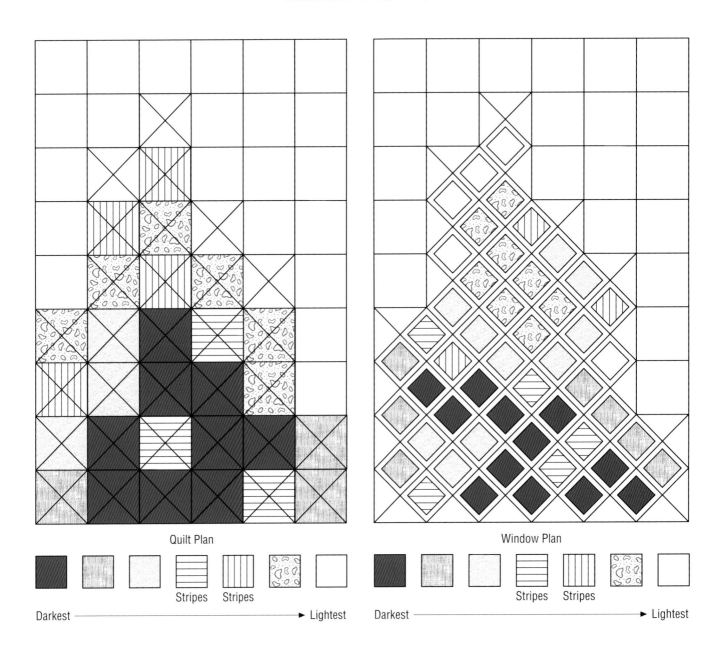

Quilt Plan

Darkest ——————————————————→ Lightest

Stripes   Stripes

Window Plan

Darkest ——————————————————→ Lightest

Stripes   Stripes

This design does not have to be slavishly copied. It can be used as a starting point for your own flowing design. Select the fabrics for the tower and make them into folded squares. Spend some time arranging these until you get the effect you want. You may have to supplement some squares and discard others. This is where a pin board or design wall is really useful, so you can pin the squares up on a surface, then stand back to get the full effect of the

design as it develops. Once your tower is to your liking, cut windows and pin them in place. Don't join the base squares in case you need to make design changes. This is not a stage that can be rushed, but it is an absolutely fascinating process!

When you finally reach the point where you feel comfortable with what you see and the balance feels good (in other words, when you can look at it and think "yes!"), make a plan of your design before you start to dismantle it for stitching. There are no rigid rules for all this. I like to get the main area, in this case, the tower, stitched together and the windows in place before I agonize over the background. I have usually sorted out the colours and general shading, but I leave the exact positioning until later. Through experience, I have found that if I plan the whole thing in great detail, I usually have to change it all as the design develops.

Working the way I do makes joining the background Secret Garden squares to the Cathedral Window tower more awkward, as the principle of stitching in straight rows cannot be followed. It's the price I have to pay for wanting my tower complete before working on the background. I still work in rows as much as I can—it's just getting 'round the corners that is a little more fiddly.

You may prefer to make up all the background squares and pin them in position on your design wall before joining anything. Try to remain flexible about how you approach your work; what is comfortable for you is what you want, and never mind how anyone else works.

Materials

(44"-wide fabric)

1½ yds. total of 7 different fabrics in gradated colours from dark to light for Cathedral Window background squares*

1 yd. for Secret Garden background squares

½ yd. total assorted scraps for windows

½ yd. for border

¾ yd. for backing

½ yd. of 2-ounce batting

¼ yd. for binding

* Use for the windows in the tower and for the Secret Garden windows in the background if you wish.

Cutting and Block Construction

1. Cut a total of 32 squares, each 6½" x 6½", from the 7 gradated fabrics for the Cathedral Window tower. Construct these squares and arrange them, following the quilt plan. (Or, you may find that a different arrangement suits your fabrics better. Pin them up on your design wall and move them about until you are satisfied with your design.)

2. After pinning each background square for the tower in place, make a window template by tracing the appropriate square on page 13 for a 3" folded square, or rotary cut the window squares if you prefer.

3. Following the window plan on page 34, cut a total of 50 windows from 7 fabrics of different shades and arrange them on the background squares.

Note

I used silk fabrics in this wall hanging and was able to obtain even subtler shades by turning the squares in different directions to change the colour slightly. You may well make changes to this initial design of the windows when you see the effect that your own range of fabric makes. Move them about until you are quite happy with the design.

4. Draw a plan as a guide for positioning the squares of the tower before removing the folded squares and windows row by row.

5. Join the squares in rows, adding the windows as you go. After completing the tower assembly, pin it to the design wall and turn your attention to the background.

6. For the Secret Garden background squares, cut 22 squares of the chosen fabric, each 6½" x 6½". Finished squares will measure 3" x 3".

7. Using 3 gradated shades of fabric for the windows as shown below, cut 6 windows, each measuring 3" x 3" from the lightest fabric, 7 windows from the middle shade, and 9 windows from the darkest shade.

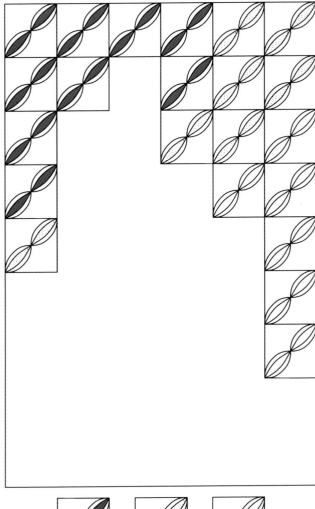

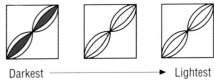

Darkest ⎯⎯⎯⎯⎯⎯→ Lightest

8. Assemble each Secret Garden square and add its window, following the directions on page 24 but turning back only 2 of the petal shapes. This forms a diagonal design rather than a floral shape as in the traditional design. Anchor the unopened edges with a bar tack through all layers about ¼" from the corners.

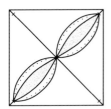

Quilt Top Assembly and Finishing

1. Following the quilt plan, arrange the 22 Secret Garden squares in position around the tower on your design wall. If you pin everything in place before you sew, you have the chance to change the arrangement if you need to for the best effect.

2. Once you are satisfied with your background squares, stitch them together in rows and join them row by row to the central tower.

3. Following the directions beginning on page 97, measure, cut, back with batting, and add mitered borders to the quilt top. Cut border strips and batting strips 4" wide.

4. Back the quilt and tie at regular intervals to hold the layers together, referring to the directions on page 99.

5. Quilt the borders with diagonal rows of stitching spaced 3" apart.

6. Bind the edges.

Exploring

New

Shapes

Traditionally, the Cathedral Window design has been based on individual folded squares joined into rows or blocks. The potential for developing designs and movement is greatly increased if the squares are combined with rectangles in much the same way as they are used in pieced patchwork blocks. A few of the infinite number of possible combinations of square and rectangle windows are shown here.

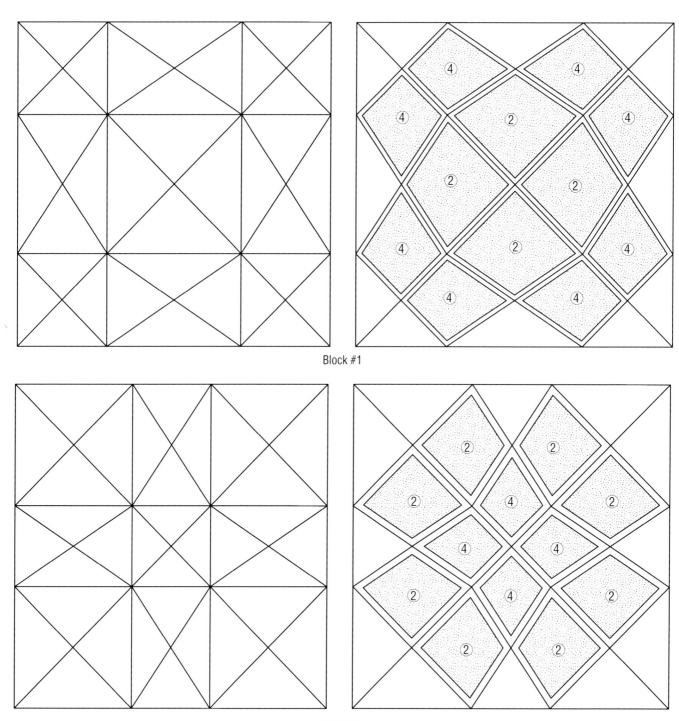

Block #1

Block #2

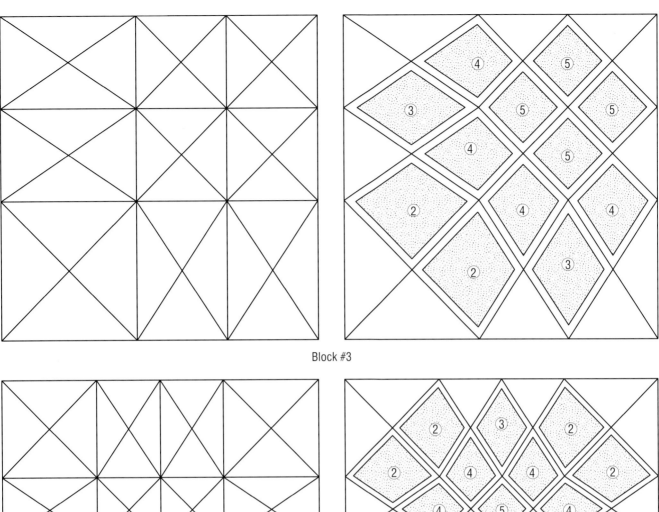

Block #3

Block #4

All of these designs were drawn using squares with a rectangle that is 1½ times the width of the smaller square (or the side of the square). If the square measures 3" x 3", the rectangle measures 3" x 4½". The larger squares in the designs then must measure 4½" to match the long side of the rectangle.

This rectangle is a good shape to try from the start, as the distortion of the windows is not too extreme and good results are possible without much difficulty. The numbers in each window refer to the window template required for the resulting shapes. These templates appear on page 55.

Drafting the Rectangle Template

The template for a rectangular Cathedral Window unit is not the rectangle that you would expect it to be. Instead, it is a very odd shape indeed. See page 54. To create it, the best way is to draw out the final shape and work back through the folding procedures until you get the required template shape.

1. Draw the desired finished rectangle full size on graph paper. Draw diagonal lines from corner to corner. This is what the folded fabric rectangle will look like after you have finished folding it.

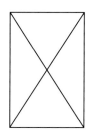

2. Draw a horizontal and vertical line through the center of the rectangle and well beyond it. Measure from the center (O) to point A and mark this distance from A to AA and from C to CC. Measure from the center (O) to point B and mark this distance from B to BB and from D to DD.

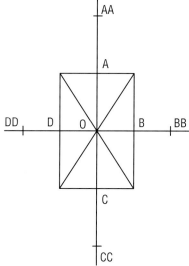

3. Join the 4 points AA, BB, CC, and DD to form a diamond.

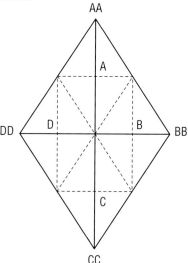

4. Trace the diamond onto a fresh piece of graph paper. Draw a vertical and a horizontal line through the center of the diamond.

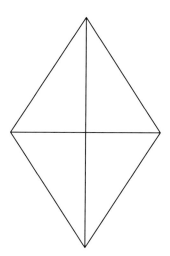

5. Make a plastic or stiff paper template of one triangular quarter of the diamond. Flip this over and place the longest edge against one side of the diamond. Draw around the other two sides. Repeat this on the remaining 3 sides of the diamond. This makes the complete shape for a rectangular Cathedral Window template. See the illustration above right.

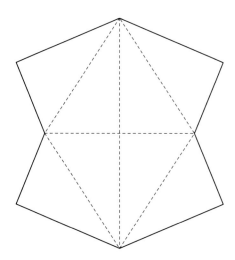

6. Add a ¼"-wide seam allowance all around the shape to complete the template.

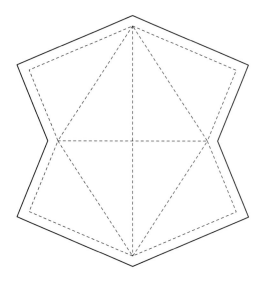

Constructing the Rectangle

The resulting template is not at all the simple shape one would expect and can only be folded into the required rectangle by using the machine-stitching technique, not by folding and pressing.

1. Make a template by tracing Template #1 on page 54 (or other rectangle template of the desired size) onto template plastic. You may glue your graph-paper shape to a piece of lightweight cardboard if you prefer. Draw around it on the back of the fabric and cut out.

2. Fold the fabric in half with right sides together along line A/B. Machine stitch the short edges together, using a ¼"-wide seam as shown.

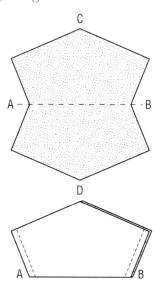

3. Open out and fold from point C to point D, matching the seams in the center. Starting about 1" from the center, machine stitch to point C, then backstitch 2 or 3 stitches to secure, stitching forward again and off the end of the fabric. Clip the threads, leaving a long length of top and bobbin threads at point C. Repeat from the center to point D.

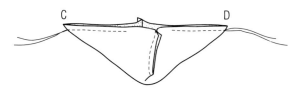

4. Trim the corners at points C and D to reduce the bulk in the seam allowances. Press the 4 seams open with the point of the iron and try not to press a crease in the outer edges of the folded, kitelike envelope.

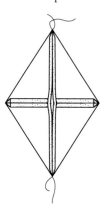

5. Turn the envelope right side out.

Tip

To make it easier to pull the corners out smoothly at Points C and D, insert the thread tails into a large-eyed needle. Insert the needle in the fabric as near to the end of the stitching at one corner as possible. Pull the corner through to its right side with the needle and threads. Repeat at the other corner. Clip the threads.

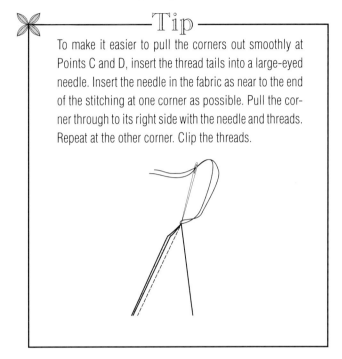

6. Press the shape, then close the opening in the center of the seam with 2 or 3 tiny stitches, beginning and ending on the back of the piece. Leave the thread and needle attached for the next step.

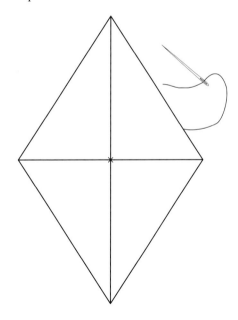

7. Bring each corner in to the center in turn, pressing firmly and keeping the outside corners as sharp as possible. Using the original thread, stitch the center down firmly through all layers and fasten off at the back, as for the classic Cathedral Window (page 12).

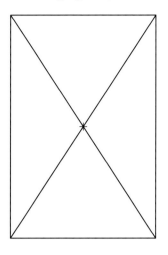

Using Rectangles with Squares

It is important to keep the measurement of the final folded squares and rectangles accurate. Check them as you construct them, especially if you have folded them using the iron instead of by machine stitching them. If you are preparing background squares by hand, turn under a scant ¼" in the second step (page 10) to ensure that the final folded square is 3" x 3" and not smaller.

Matching squares and rectangles is quite simple: the smaller square links with itself and with the short side of the rectangle; the large square links with itself and with the long side of the rectangle.

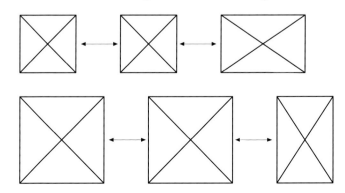

Adding Windows

A variety of window shapes occurs, depending on which folded shapes are stitched together. All of the window templates for rectangles for the projects in this book are included. To make window templates for other shapes in projects of your own design, stitch the folded shapes together and trace the four-sided shape formed over two adjoining envelopes. This may be symmetrical or asymmetrical as shown in the two examples below. Trim the shape down by about ⅛".

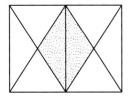 

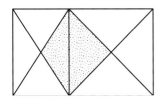

Creating Accurate Windows

I dealt with the art of stitching corners when sewing in the windows, beginning on page 13. The corners of windows that are other than simple squares present new problems. Some corners will be wider than 90°. When making the bartack stitches across these corners, the fabric must be pulled across the windows firmly, as the two bias edges have to stretch across the wider angle of the corner. Be careful not to trim the window fabric too much in case it frays out at this corner.

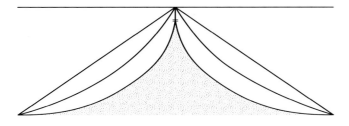

When turned, the seam allowances in the sharper, narrower corner are compressed inside and tend to be bulky. This makes it difficult to turn the edges neatly over the window. Use the side of a small pair of scissors to press down the center of the pointed corner to help persuade it to turn with both sides balanced.

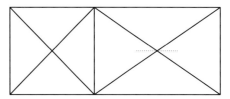

Press firmly along dotted line.

Even with this assistance, the turned edges will not lie completely flat. Usually they make a slight petal shape beyond the bar tack. This cannot be avoided, so just make sure the petal shapes balance on each side and that no tufts of window fabric show in this petal.

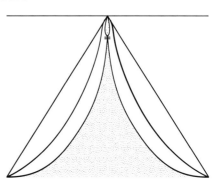

Designing with Three Shapes

Any of the arrangements of large squares, small squares, and rectangles shown in the four designs on pages 38–39 can be used as blocks and combined with sashing in a quilt. Block #3 has a strong diagonal emphasis and can be used as a repeating block in a variety of ways. The photos at the bottom of the page show this same block interpreted in fabric in two different ways. The first block has one fabric only for the background folded shapes and hand-dyed cotton fabric in the windows. The second block features three fabrics in the background and a variety of silks in the windows. The illustration below is a representation of the second block. The numbers refer to the window templates required for the resulting shapes. These templates appear on page 55.

creating a three-dimensional effect. If the small squares are grouped in the center, the effect is of depth in the central area. See illustrations below.

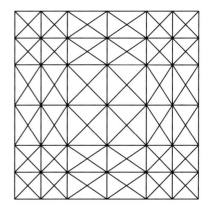

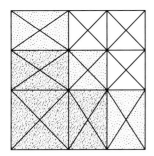 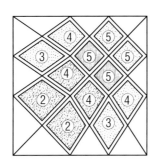

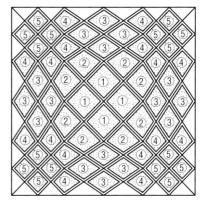

Four of these blocks can be combined to make a larger design. If the large squares are placed in the center, the central windows seem to curve outward,

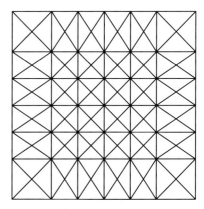

Block One (left) by Lynne Edwards, 1994, Suffolk, England, 13" x 13". This design combines rectangles, small squares, and one large square.

Block Two by Lynne Edwards, 1994, Suffolk, England, 10¼" x 10¼". The same block design done on a smaller scale, features three textured fabrics in the folded squares.

Shades of Gill *by Lynne Edwards, 1994, Suffolk, England, 35" x 35". This subtly shaded quilt has a strong central focus, created through the use of large folded squares.*

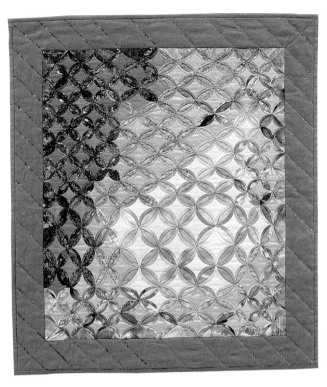

Dawn to Dusk *by Lynne Edwards, 1989, Suffolk, England, 34" x 40½". Silk windows in many shades move the colour across the surface of this quilt built on textured background squares.*

This illusion was developed in the quilt "Shades of Gill." It was named for friend and student Gill Sharman, whose liking for weary shades of mauves and grays is as odd as my own colour preferences. Complete directions for this quilt begin on page 48.

The wall hanging "Dawn to Dusk" is composed of just three different shapes—a small square, a rectangle, and a large square. The background in this quilt was made from four very textured fabrics. Two are from the exciting range of designer patchwork fabrics, one is hand-dyed, and the fourth is a decorator fabric (called a furnishing cotton in England), which has streaks and splashes of silver in it. I'd describe this fabric as "a bit over the top" for curtains, but wonderful for a Cathedral Window quilt!

The silk windows range in colour shades from silvery to deep, dark blue. I was aiming for an Impressionistic effect of shading and movement that would shift from the dawn's light to dusk. For the borders, I chose a damask linen that I quilted with decorative stitches and silver couching.

A focus of light in the center of the background folded shapes moves outward, becoming darker to-

ward the top left side. The windows follow the same route. I used seven shades of silk and also created subtle variations in shading by turning the silk 180°.

When a design is destined for the wall as opposed to the bed, you can really set aside the hard-wearing aspect and concentrate on the visual effect. You can mix different fabrics and use exciting threads when you feel like it. Complete directions for "Dawn to Dusk" begin on page 50.

Using Longer Rectangles

A more distorted shape can be achieved by using a longer rectangle, one that is twice as long as it is wide. This more extreme shape is developed in exactly the same way as the shorter rectangle already discussed. The double-length rectangle can be used with large and small squares to make many interesting and exciting designs.

A template for a long rectangle that measures 3" x 6" appears on page 56. If you wish to draft templates for other rectangle sizes, follow the steps for "Drafting the Rectangle Template" on page 40.

The longer the rectangle, the narrower and wider the corner points will be. Follow the directions on page 43, "Creating Accurate Windows" for handling these types of corners.

In the "Silver Birch Quilt," a dense grid of squares and rectangles in the center area extends outward with large squares to make a stepped diamond shape of Cathedral Window units. The quilted border squares off the quilt and frames the center diamond.

You can use the double-length rectangle with shorter rectangles to create subtle distortion of the window shapes.

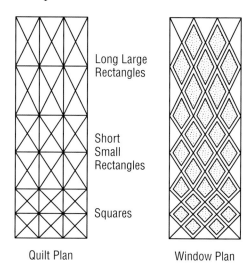

Long Large Rectangles

Short Small Rectangles

Squares

Quilt Plan   Window Plan

Experiment with these shapes. Many wonderful combinations are possible. If the windows turn out to be very odd shapes, trace them from the joined folded squares and rectangles and make templates from these shapes, trimming them down by about ⅛". The windows can be more accurately trimmed once they are pinned in place ready for stitching.

Silver Birch Quilt *by Lynne Edwards, 1989, Suffolk, England, 53" x 53". I used a patterned polished cotton fabric with windows of silk in gray and green to make this tranquil quilt.*

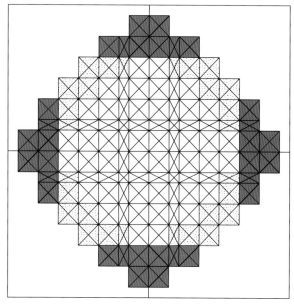

Quilt Plan for "Silver Birch Quilt"

Window Plan

Using Even Longer Rectangles

"Movement," shown below, is a wall hanging that relies on a variety of squares and rectangles to create movement. The focus is a large square surrounded by short rectangles (4" x 6" finished) and by 4" squares. More depth was created at the top and bottom by using rectangles that are only 2" wide. This means that, in some places, the finished rectangles measure 2" x 6" (that is, the length is 3 times longer than the width).

As this rectangle is even narrower and more distorted than the double-length rectangle, take care during construction to keep the corners as balanced and as flat as possible. Refer to the discussion of double-length rectangles on page 45. Complete directions for this quilt begin on page 52.

"Shades of Houston," shown below right, is another wall hanging that requires several sizes of squares and rectangles. I made it after my first trip to Houston, Texas, where I was overwhelmed by the colours and reflections of the buildings in the center

of the city. It has two points of focus highlighted by areas of folded marbled fabric that move out into silver grays and blues. The windows are of many shades of silk, matching as nearly as possible the colours of the metal and glass of the buildings. They move out from the two focal points in circles and then sweep across the quilt in curving lines to give a feeling of movement.

The illustration below shows how these folded background shapes have been arranged.

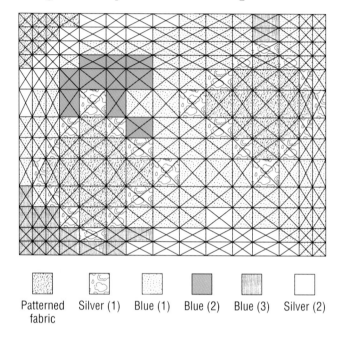

| Patterned fabric | Silver (1) | Blue (1) | Blue (2) | Blue (3) | Silver (2) |

Movement *by Lynne Edwards, 1989, Suffolk, England, 32" x 36". Glowing shades of yellow and gold move across the surface of this small wall hanging. Owned by Hazel Hurst.*

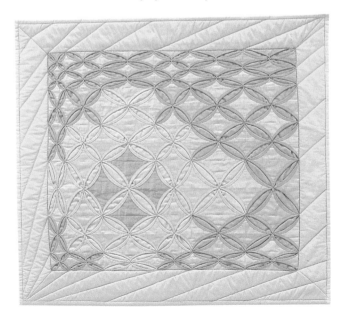

Shades of Houston *by Lynne Edwards, 1993, Suffolk, England, 57" x 72½". The colors and reflections of the buildings in Houston, Texas, were the inspiration for this quilt. Squares and rectangles of different sizes help create the feeling of space and movement. Owned by Rosemary Wilkinson.*

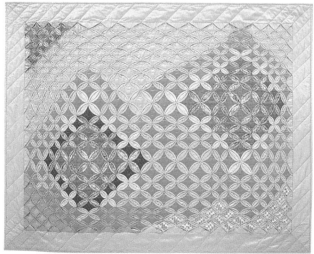

SHADES OF GILL

Colour photo on page 45
Finished Quilt Size: 35" x 35"

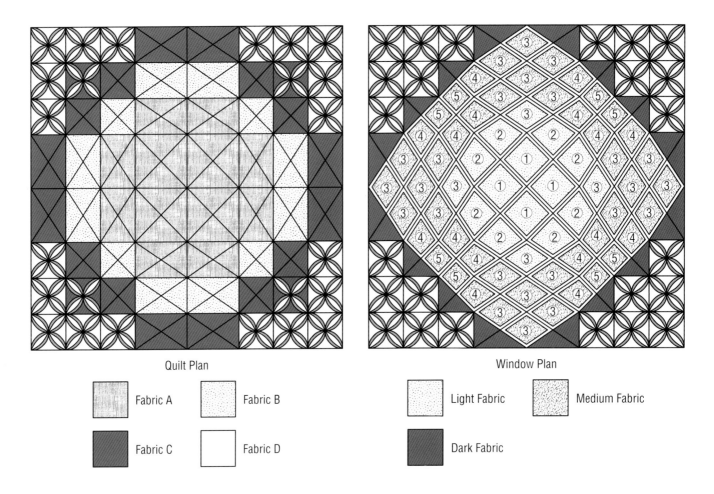

Quilt Plan

Fabric A

Fabric B

Fabric C

Fabric D

Window Plan

Light Fabric

Medium Fabric

Dark Fabric

This design requires three different folded shapes—a large square that finishes to 4½" x 4½", a small square that finishes to 3" x 3", and a rectangle that is 3" x 4½". The central design is composed of Cathedral Window units, while the corners are Secret Garden squares, each measuring 3" x 3".

Materials

(44"-wide fabric)

1⅛ yds. Fabric A for background squares
¾ yd. Fabric B for background squares
1 yd. Fabric C for background squares
¾ yd. Fabric D for background squares
½ yd. each of 3 shades (light, medium, dark) of silk for windows
½ yd. silk in a tone that blends with Fabric D for border
1 yd. for backing
1 yd. of 2-ounce batting
¼ yd. for binding

Cutting and Block Construction

1. Referring to the quilt plan, cut the required pieces from the following fabrics. Use Template #1 on page 54 to cut the pieces for all rectangular background pieces.

   Fabric A
       4 squares, each 9½" x 9½"
       8 Template #1 for the rectangles

   Fabric B
       4 small squares, each 6½" x 6½"
       8 Template #1 for the rectangles

   Fabric C
       12 squares, each 6½" x 6½"
       8 Template #1 for the rectangles

   Fabric D
       20 squares, each 6½" x 6½"

2. Construct the Cathedral Window folded background squares and rectangles of Fabrics A and B. Construct all the rectangles and 8 of the Fabric C squares. Follow the directions for "Making Classic Cathedral Windows," beginning on page 10, and the directions for rectangular windows, beginning on page 41.

3. Use the remaining 4 squares of Fabric C and all 20 squares of Fabric D for the required Secret Garden squares. For the windows in the Secret Garden squares, cut 24 squares, each 3" x 3", from your silk window fabrics. Refer to the window plan on page 48. Construct the 24 Secret Garden squares with their hidden windows as shown on page 24. The finished squares will measure 3" x 3".

Quilt Top Assembly and Finishing

1. Following the quilt plan, arrange the folded Cathedral Window squares and rectangles with the Secret Garden squares.

2. Join the squares and rectangles in rows. Stitch the rows together to form the block, matching seams carefully.

Tip
With a design like this one, I like to join the center block of squares and rectangles together with their windows and then work outwards, adding the windows as I go.

3. Make templates for the windows by tracing the 5 shapes on page 55 (Templates #1–#5).

4. Following the window plan on page 48, use Template #1 to cut 4 windows from your chosen silk for the center. Pin and sew these in position, taking care to keep the grain of the silk in the same direction, or the colour will not appear to be the same.

5. Use the same silk for the surrounding ring of windows, but turn it 90° when cutting so that it appears to be a slightly different colour. (Or, use another colour altogether.) Cut and stitch in position: 8 windows from Template #2 and 4 windows from Template #3.

6. Using another shade of silk, cut and stitch in position: 12 windows from Template #3 and 8 windows from Template #4.

7. Turn the same silk fabric 90° for the next round of windows to create a subtle difference in shade. (Or, use another colour of silk.) Cut and stitch in position: 12 windows from Template #3; 8 windows from Template #4; and 8 windows from Template #5.

8. Complete each corner with 5 Secret Garden squares cut from Fabric D and 1 Secret Garden square cut from Fabric C.

9. Following the directions beginning on page 97, measure, cut, back with batting, and add mitered borders to the quilt top. Cut border strips and batting strips 4" wide.

10. Back the quilt and tie at regular intervals to hold the layers together, referring to the directions on page 99.

11. Quilt the borders diagonally at 3" intervals as shown in the photo on page 45.

12. Bind the edges.

DAWN TO DUSK
Colour photo on page 45
Finished Quilt Size: 34" x 40½"

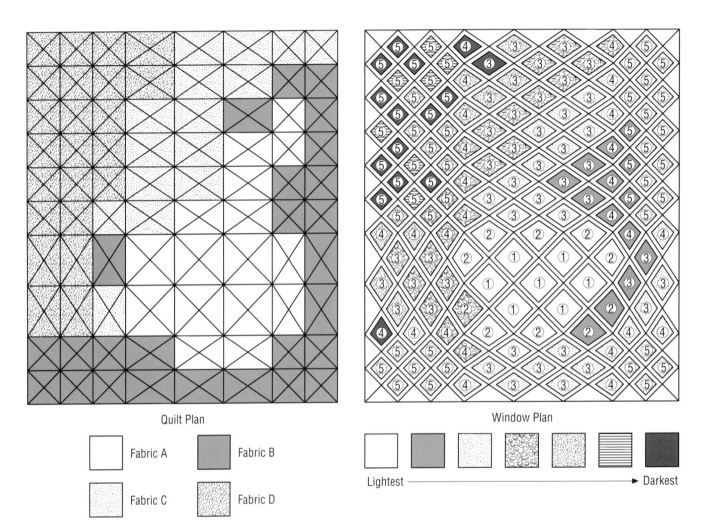

Quilt Plan

☐ Fabric A ▨ Fabric B

▨ Fabric C ▨ Fabric D

Window Plan

Lightest ⟶ Darkest

Use this design as a starting point for your own ideas. Much will depend on the fabric you collect for the project. Pin the folded shapes into place on a design wall. Add or discard some as needed.

Once the background layout is to your liking, cut windows and pin them in place. Don't rush. Getting something right usually takes time. Get on with other things but look at the design as you walk past it, pinning on a couple of windows and letting it cook for a while as you ponder the effect. When you feel comfortable with what you see, make a plan of the design before dismantling it.

It's easier to stitch a piece this size in sections, because the windows are easier to reach and the weight of all those folded fabrics is considerable.

Materials

(44"-wide fabrics)
1 yd. each of 4 different fabrics
for background shapes
Approximately 1 yd. total of 7 fabrics
in gradated shades for windows
(Window Fabrics #1–#7)
½ yd. for border
1 yd. for backing
½ yd. of 2-ounce batting
¼ yd. for binding

Cutting and Block Construction

1. Referring to the quilt plan, cut the required pieces from the following fabrics. Use Template #1 on page 54 to cut the pieces for all rectangular background pieces.

    Fabric A
        6 squares, each 9½" x 9½"
        8 Template #1 for rectangles
        2 squares, each 6½" x 6½"
    Fabric B
        8 Template #1 for rectangles
        18 squares, each 6½" x 6½"
    Fabric C
        12 Template #1 for rectangles
        3 squares, each 6½" x 6½"
    Fabric D
        6 Template #1 for rectangles
        17 squares, each 6½" x 6½"

2. Construct the Cathedral Window folded squares and rectangles from each fabric, following the directions for Cathedral Window, beginning on page 10, and the directions for rectangular windows, beginning on page 41.

3. Pin the completed units in place on your design wall to make sure that you like the effect. Make any desired design alterations at this stage.

Quilt Top Assembly and Finishing

1. Referring to the quilt plan for placement, join the squares and rectangles into rows. Stitch the rows together, matching seams carefully.

2. Make templates for the windows by tracing the 5 shapes on page 55 (Templates #1–#5).

3. Assign a number to each of the window fabrics, beginning with the lightest and working toward the darkest shade.

4. Following the window plan on page 50 and using Fabric #1, cut:
        7 windows from Template #1
        7 windows from Template #2
        4 windows from Template #3
    Pin and stitch these in position.

Tip

If you are using silk for the windows, take care to keep the grain of the fabric in the same direction or the colour will not appear to be the same. I use this changeable nature of silk fabrics by consciously arranging some of the windows with the grain in the other direction to add another shade to the design.

5. Using Fabric #2, cut and stitch in position:
        2 windows from Template #2
        5 windows from Template #3
        4 windows from Template #4
        3 windows from Template #5

6. Using Fabric #3, cut and stitch in position:
        16 windows from Template #3
        9 windows from Template #4
        24 windows from Template #5

7. Using Fabric #4, cut and stitch in position:
        1 window from Template #2
        13 windows from Template #3
        7 windows from Template #4
        2 windows from Template #5

8. Using Fabric #5, cut and stitch in position:
        5 windows from Template #3
        4 windows from Template #4
        6 windows from Template #5

9. From Fabric #6, cut and stitch in position:
        1 window from Template #3
        7 windows from Template #5

10. From Fabric #7, cut and stitch in position:
        1 window from Template #3
        2 windows from Template #4
        12 windows from Template #5

11. Following the directions beginning on page 97, measure, cut, back with batting, and add mitered borders to the quilt top. Cut border strips and batting strips 4½" wide.

12. Back the quilt and tie at regular intervals to hold the layers together, referring to the directions on page 99. Quilt the border if desired.

13. Bind the edges.

MOVEMENT

Colour photo on page 47
Finished Quilt Size: 32" x 36"

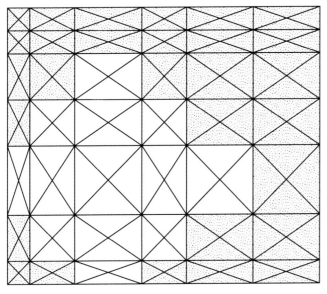

Quilt Plan

☐ Fabric A   ▦ Fabric B

Window Plan

Darkest ──────────────▶ Lightest

Materials

(44"-wide fabrics)
1 yd. Fabric A
1¾ yds. Fabric B
¼ yd. each of 5 silk fabrics in
gradated shades for windows
½ yd. for border
1 yd. for backing
1 yd. of 2-ounce batting
¼ yd. for binding

Use the shapes shown at right to create this quilt.
Rectangle templates are on pages 57–59.

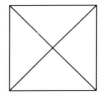

6" square (cut 12½")

4" square (cut 8½")

2" square (cut 4½")

4" x 6" short rectangle
(Template 5, page 59)

2" x 4" double length rectangle
(Template 4, page 58)

2" x 6" triple length rectangle
(Template 3, page 57)

Cutting and Block Construction

Refer to the quilt plan as you cut and prepare the background units. Use rectangle templates on pages 57–59.

1. From Fabric A, cut and construct:
   2 folded squares, each 6" x 6"
      (12½" x 12½" cut size)
   4 folded squares, each 4" x 4"
      (8½" x 8½" cut size)
   5 folded short rectangles
      (Rectangle Template #5),
      each 4" x 6" finished
   2 folded triple-rectangles
      (Rectangle Template #3),
      each 2" x 6" finished

2. From Fabric B, cut and construct:
   1 folded square, 6" x 6"
      (12½" x 12½" cut size)
   2 folded squares, each 4" x 4"
      (8½" x 8½" cut size)
   3 folded squares, each 2" x 2"
      (4½" x 4½" cut size)
   6 folded short rectangles
      (Rectangle Template #5),
      each 4" x 6" finished
   9 folded double-length rectangles
      (Rectangle Template #4),
      each 2" x 4" finished
   8 folded triple-length rectangles
      (Rectangle Template #3),
      each 2" x 6" finished

Quilt Top Assembly

1. Stitch the completed shapes together in rows as shown in the quilt plan, matching seams carefully. You may prefer to keep the design in two parts, stitching in as many windows as you can in each section before joining them together and adding the final row of windows.

2. Referring to the window plan on page 52 and the window identification key, above right, cut and stitch the windows, using 5 shades of silk, gradating from the darkest out to the lightest. Templates for the various window shapes required appear on pages 60–63.

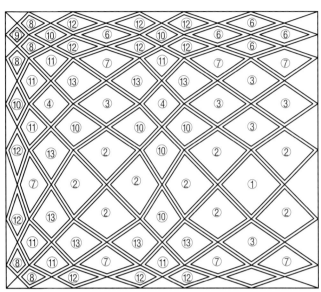

Window Identification Key

3. Following the directions beginning on page 97, measure, cut, back with batting, and add mitered borders to the quilt top. Cut border strips and batting strips 4½" wide.

Finishing

1. Back the quilt and tie at regular intervals to hold the layers together, referring to the directions on page 99. Space ties about every 4", locating them at the block junctions and making sure that the stitches do not show on the front of the quilt.

2. Optional: Mark quilting lines from each seam junction out to the edge of the border. Vary the angles to continue the feeling of movement from the blocks out into the border.

3. Bind the edges.

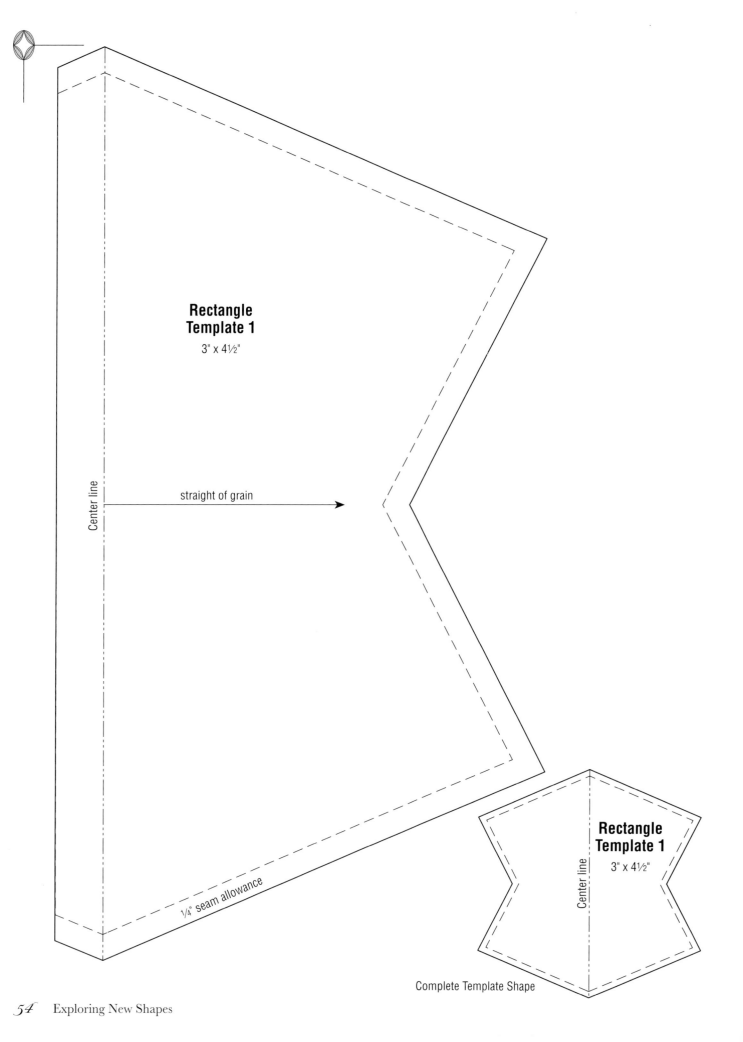

**Rectangle
Template 1**

3" x 4½"

Center line

straight of grain

¼" seam allowance

**Rectangle
Template 1**

3" x 4½"

Center line

Complete Template Shape

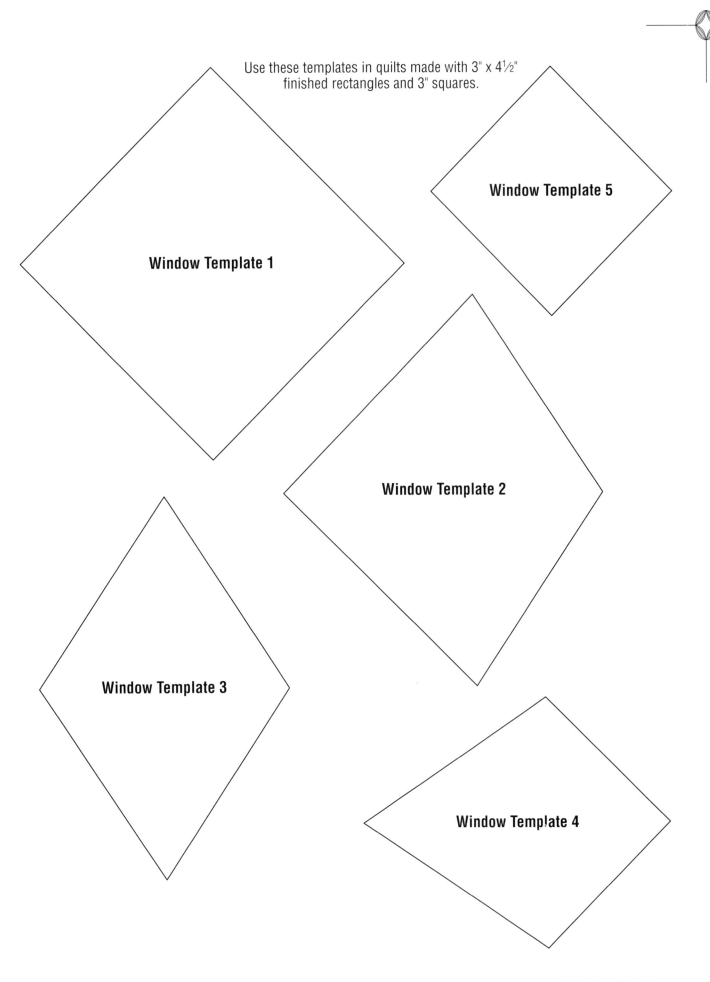

Use these templates in quilts made with 3" x 4½"
finished rectangles and 3" squares.

Window Template 1

Window Template 5

Window Template 2

Window Template 3

Window Template 4

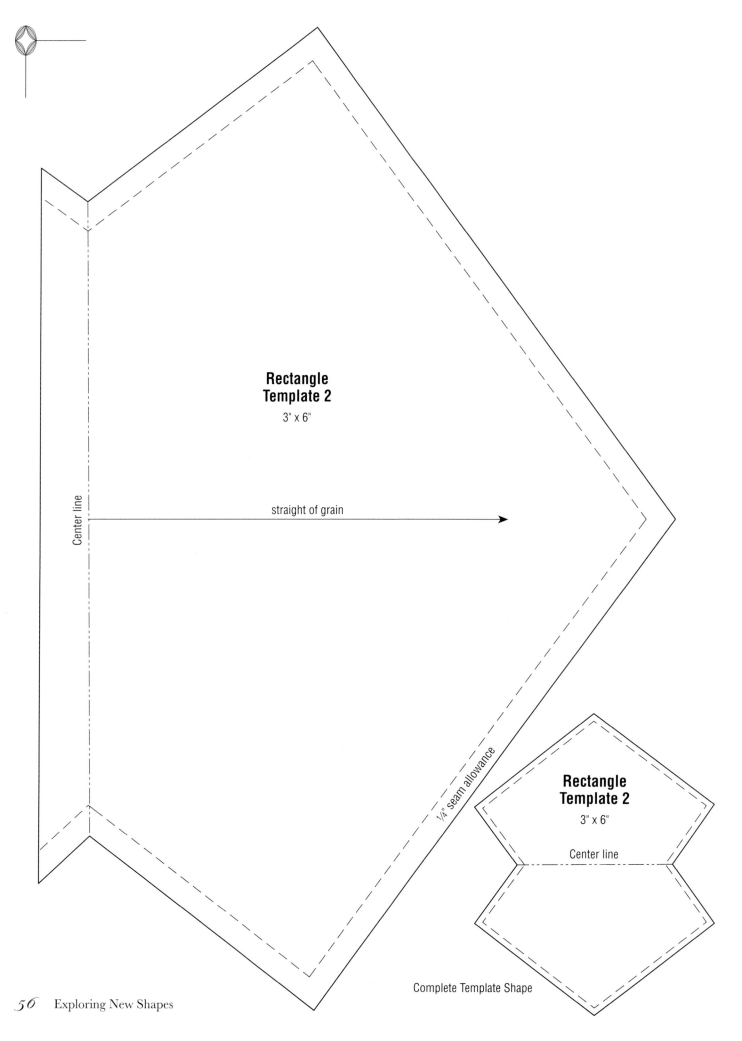

**Rectangle
Template 2**

3" x 6"

Center line

straight of grain

¼" seam allowance

**Rectangle
Template 2**

3" x 6"

Center line

Complete Template Shape

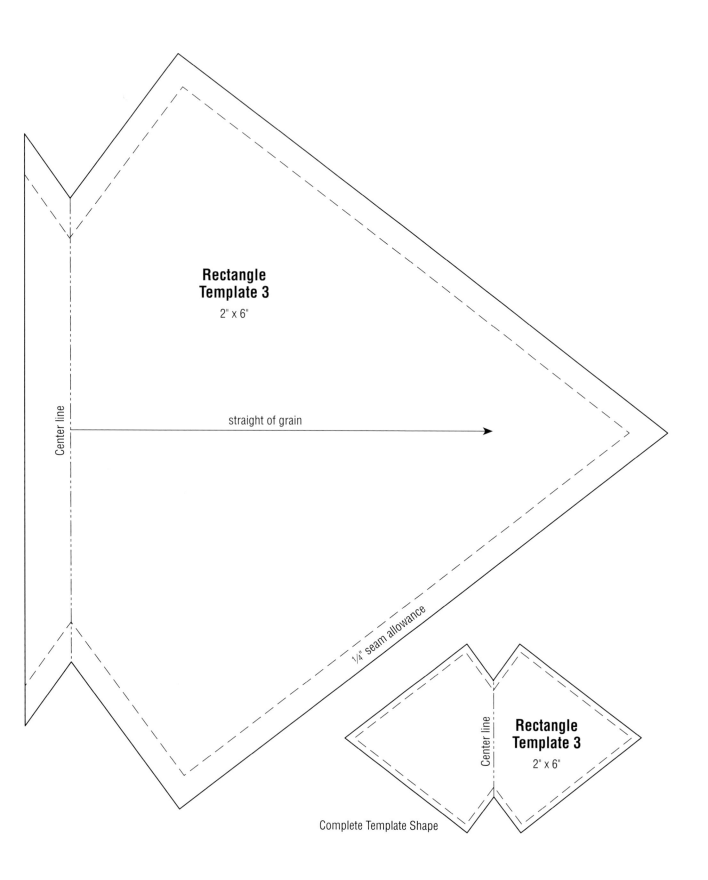

**Rectangle
Template 3**

2" x 6"

Center line

straight of grain

¼" seam allowance

Center line

**Rectangle
Template 3**

2" x 6"

Complete Template Shape

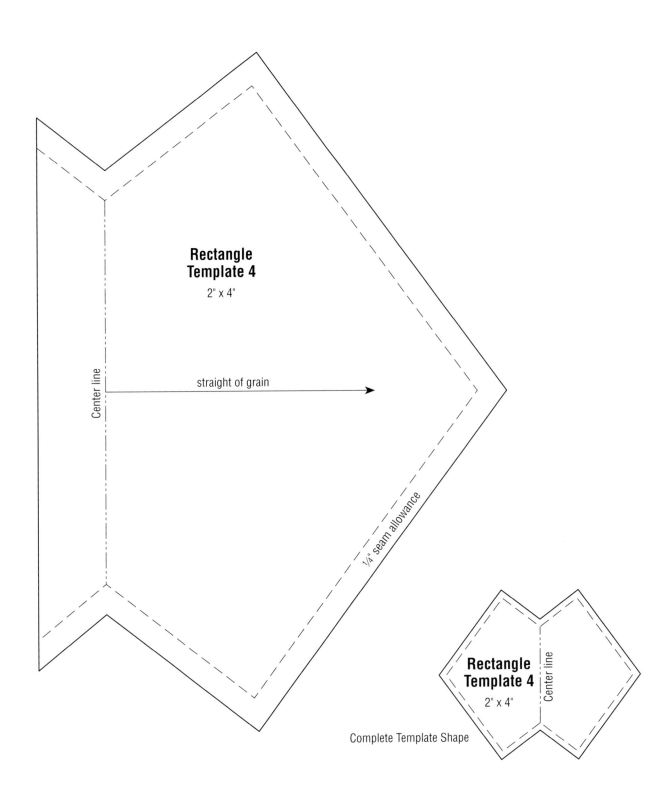

**Rectangle
Template 4**

2" x 4"

Center line

straight of grain

¼" seam allowance

**Rectangle
Template 4**

2" x 4"

Center line

Complete Template Shape

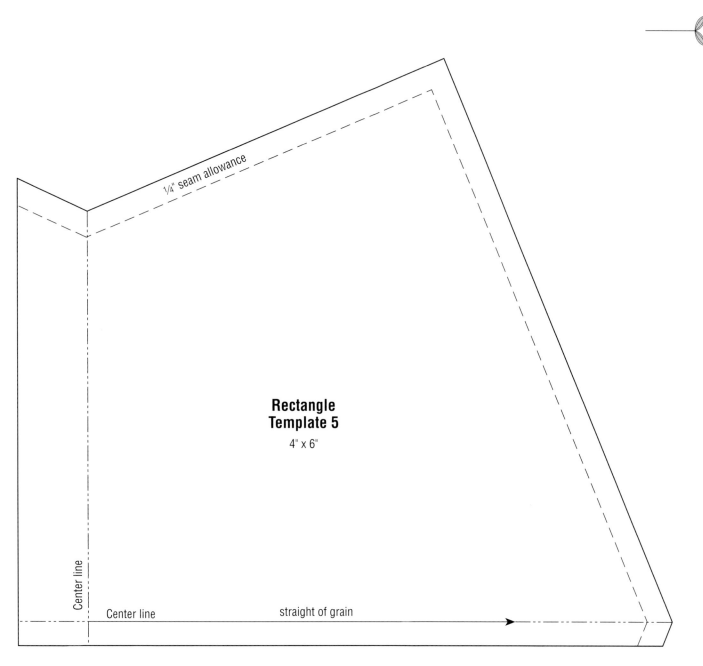

¼" seam allowance

**Rectangle
Template 5**

4" x 6"

Center line

Center line

straight of grain

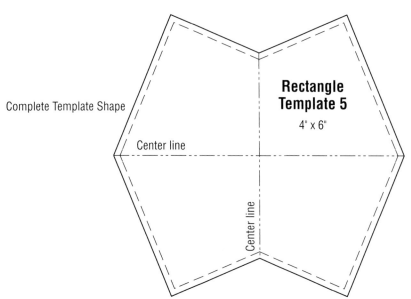

Complete Template Shape

Center line

**Rectangle
Template 5**

4" x 6"

Center line

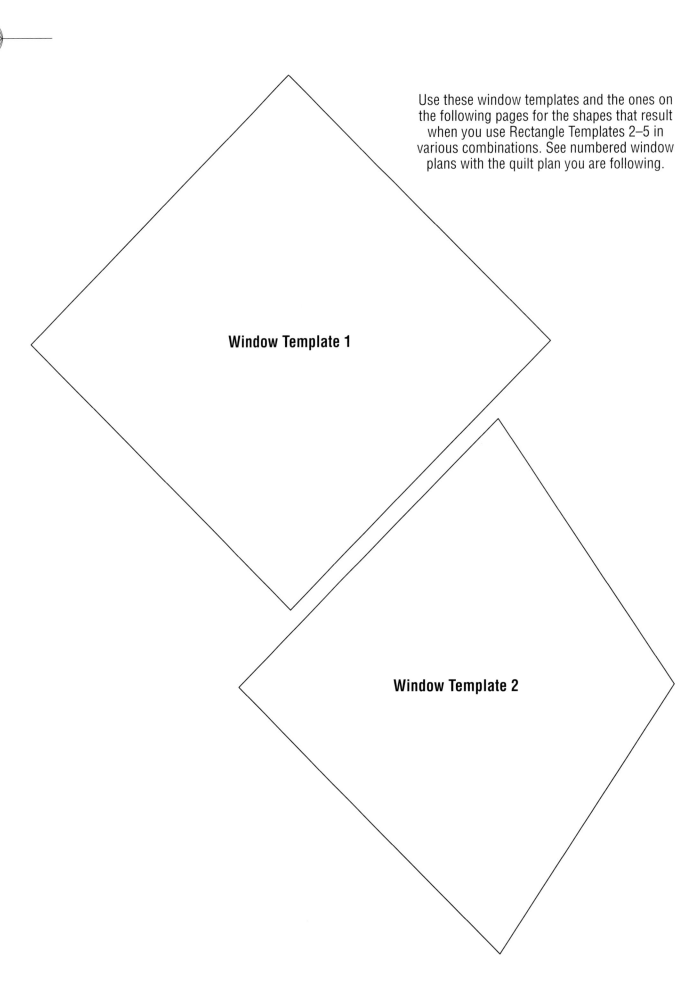

Use these window templates and the ones on the following pages for the shapes that result when you use Rectangle Templates 2–5 in various combinations. See numbered window plans with the quilt plan you are following.

Window Template 1

Window Template 2

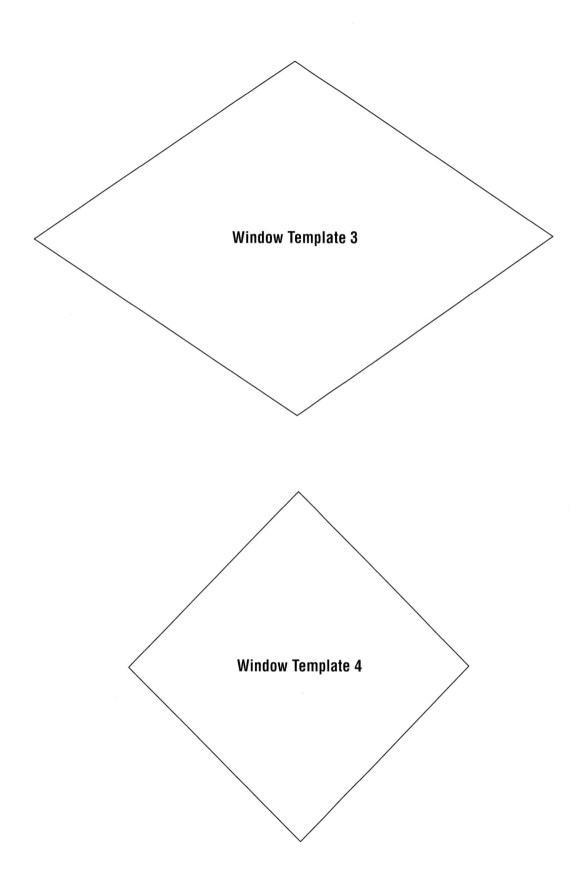

Window Template 3

Window Template 4

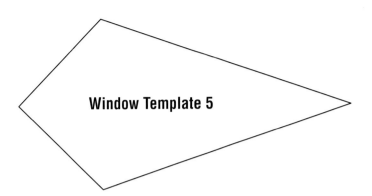

Window Template 5

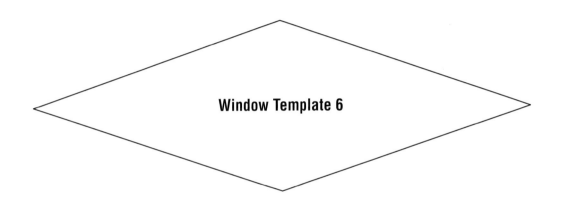

Window Template 6

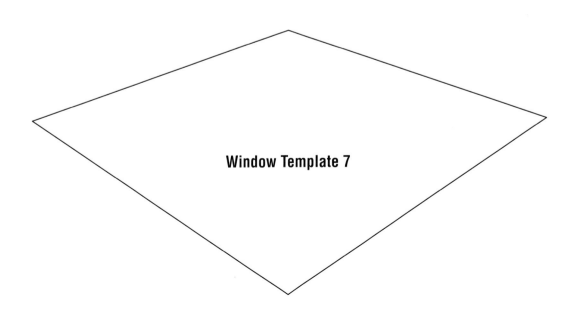

Window Template 7

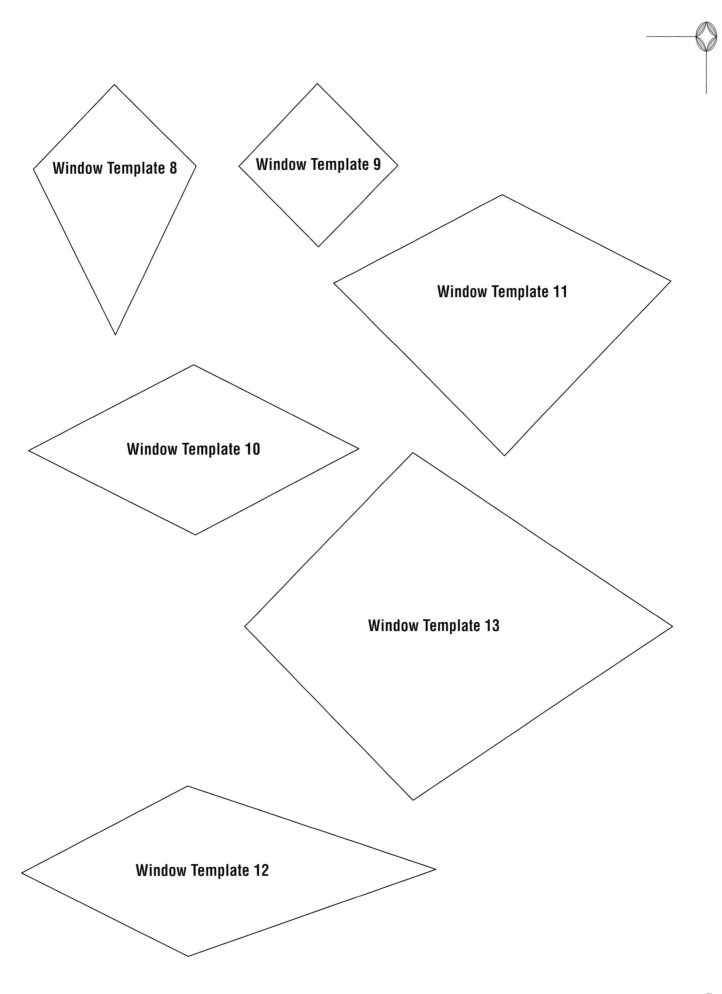

Window Template 8

Window Template 9

Window Template 11

Window Template 10

Window Template 13

Window Template 12

Expanding

Your

Design

Options

There are still two more design elements to try as you explore the exciting design possibilities of the Cathedral Window and its related shapes—Folded Triangles and Twisted Windows.

Folded Triangles

As a quilter, I am used to making blocks from squares, rectangles, and triangles, so I wondered whether it was possible to make a folded right-angle triangle. That way, I could combine two triangles to make a square. The square could then be used with other squares and rectangles for new Cathedral Window designs.

Not being a mathematician, it took me some time to find the correct starting shape that would eventually fold into a right-angle triangle. The template for such a triangle with 4"-long sides appears on page 78.

Quilts that feature folded triangle shapes include the "Nine-Block Quilt" on page 81 and the "Kingfisher Blue Hanging" on page 82. Both of these quilts feature the Nine Patch block shown below.

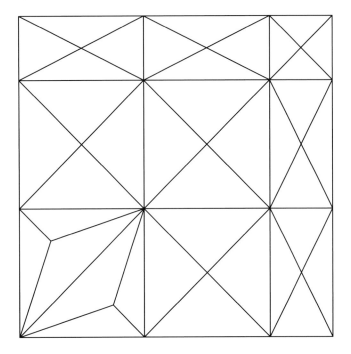

Directions for making the Nine Patch block begin on page 70. Directions for the Kingfisher wall hanging begin on page 72.

Drafting a Template for Folded Triangles

So that you may devise templates for various sizes of this unit, drafting directions appear below.

1. Draw the required finished triangle on a piece of graph paper.

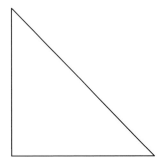

2. Mark the center of each side and draw lines from each corner of the triangle to the center mark of the opposite line. The point where the 3 lines meet marks the center of the triangle (O).

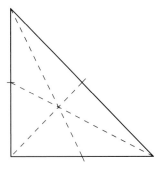

3. Referring to the illustration below, erase lines to leave just 3 triangles.

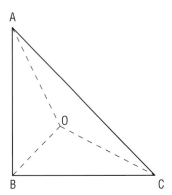

4. Trace each triangle onto stiff paper or template plastic. Cut out each shape carefully. Then place the templates in position *on* the triangle. Next,

flip each template over so its longest edge is even with the corresponding edge of the triangle. Draw around the other two sides.

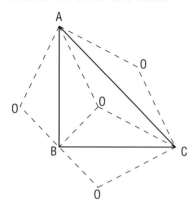

5. Carefully trace the new shape onto a fresh piece of graph paper, marking the center but omitting all other lines. Draw new lines from the center (O) to each of the corners.

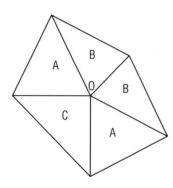

6. Trace Triangles A, B, and C to make a card or plastic template for each one. Taking each template in turn, flip it over, and place the longest edge against the matching line on the diagram. Draw around the other 2 sides. Repeat this with each template, using Triangle C once and Triangles A and B twice.

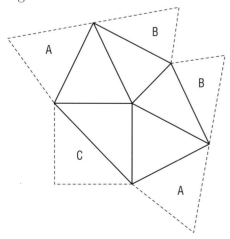

7. To this final shape, add a ¼"-wide seam allowance all around. Mark the grain line with an arrow as shown.

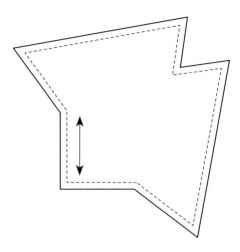

Making Folded Triangles

1. Draw around the triangle template on the wrong side of the selected fabric, matching the grain of the fabric with the grain-line arrow marked on the template. Cut out on the drawn lines.

2. Bring the 2 sides marked A together with right sides facing and stitch, using a ¼"-wide seam allowance.

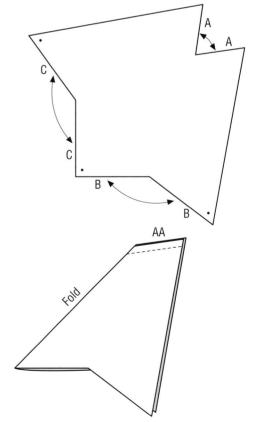

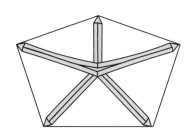

3. Repeat with the sides marked B, stitching from the fold to a point ¼" from the end of the seam line.

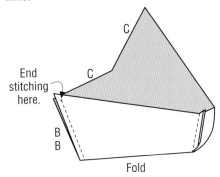

4. Repeat with the 2 sides marked C and stitch from the fold to a point ¼" from the end of the seam line.

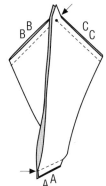

5. Open out the resulting shape and bring point AA to point BB/CC as shown. Match and pin the seams securely. Beginning about 1" from the center, stitch from the center out to the folded edge. Repeat with the remaining half of the seam.

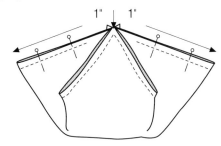

6. Trim the corners to reduce the bulk in the seam allowances. Press all 5 seams open, using the point of the iron and taking care not to press a crease in the outer edges of the folded shape.

7. Turn the shape right side out through the unstitched center. Press and sew down the center with 2 or 3 tiny stitches through all layers, starting and finishing at the back. Leave the needle and thread attached and ready for the next stage.

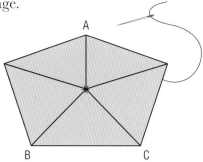

8. Bring corners A, B, and C to the center in turn, pressing firmly and keeping the outer corners as sharp as possible. Using the original thread, stitch the center down firmly through all layers and fasten off at the back as for the classic Cathedral Window (page 12). This completes the right-angle folded triangle.

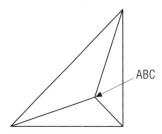

When you join two of these triangles, they make a square that you can then use alongside whole squares and rectangles to create new designs.

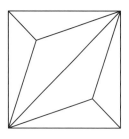

Twisted Windows

This variation of the Cathedral Window, with its folded and layered effect, has become the particular interest of quilter and friend Ann Larkin, of Suffolk, England. It is most effective when plain or lightly textured fabrics are used for the complex folding, as the folds and edges are not lost in the patterns of the fabrics. Cushions featuring Ann's Twisted Window designs appear on pages 83–84.

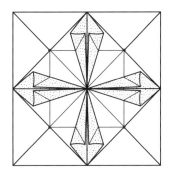

Constructing Twisted Windows

1. Construct 4 folded squares for the classic Cathedral Window in any chosen size. Refer to the directions beginning on page 10 and stop after you have completed the first stage of folding and pressing to the center and stitching in place.

Folding and Pressing Method

If using the machine-stitched envelope method shown on page 12, go as far as stitching the ends, turning the square right side out, and pressing. Stitch the center in place and also close the small opening so that the folded square is completely sealed. Keep the stitching as nearly invisible as possible, as some of these seams will show in the final design.

Machine Stitched Method

Note

If you use the machine-stitched method, the resulting designs will be more secure, while designs made using folded-and-pressed squares are more interesting, with more complex folds in the final design.

2. Next, bring each corner to the center in turn, pressing firmly and keeping the outside corners as sharp as possible. Do not stitch the center down, but pin each corner in place as shown. Repeat with each of the 4 folded squares you have prepared.

3. Join the 4 folded squares with whipstitching.

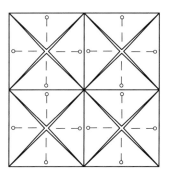

4. Remove the pins from the 8 central triangles (the shaded sections in the illustration below). Ignore these 8 flapping triangles and secure the remaining corners at the center of each folded square with a tiny pair of stitches through all layers.

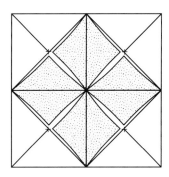

5. Referring to the illustrations below, choose one of the four folding methods. Fold the loose triangles as shown and stitch them in place after folding. Catch the loose corners with 2 tiny stitches through all layers. Press the folded block after stitching.

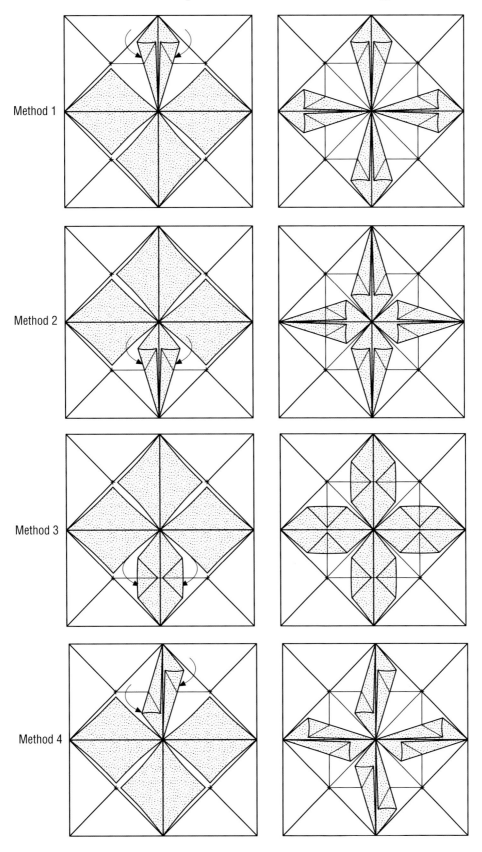

Method 1

Method 2

Method 3

Method 4

NINE PATCH BLOCK

Colour photo on page 81
Finished Quilt Size: 10" x 10"

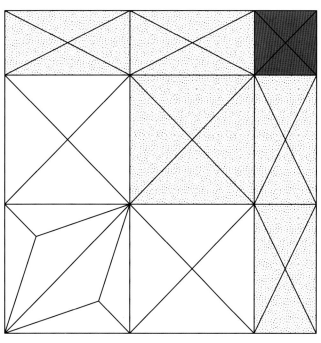

Block Plan

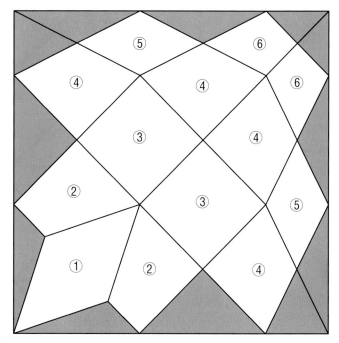

Window Plan

I combined triangles with rectangles and squares to make the Nine Patch block shown. The finished block measures 10" x 10". Make a sample block using your choice of fabric scraps to practice the technique for folded triangles (page 66). All of the folded shapes may be made from one fabric or from a combination of several as shown in the illustration.

Cutting and Construction

1. From your chosen fabrics, cut the following pieces for the background squares, rectangles, and triangles:

   2 right-angled triangles with short sides that finish to 4" (Right Triangle Template on page 78).

   3 squares, each 8½" x 8½". They will finish to 4" x 4" folded squares.

   1 small square, 4½" x 4½". It will finish to a 2" x 2" folded square.

   4 double-length rectangles, each 2" x 4" (Template #4 on page 58)

2. Construct the 2 right-angled triangles, 3 larger squares, 4 rectangles, and 1 small square, referring to the directions for Cathedral Windows, beginning on page 10, those for folded rectangles, beginning on page 41, and the ones for folded triangles, beginning on page 66.

3. Join the 2 triangles by whipstitching the two long edges together to make a square.

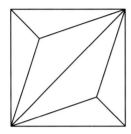

4. Referring to the block plan for placement, join the 9 shapes into 3 rows. Whipstitch the rows together, matching seams carefully to complete the block.

5. Referring to the window plan on page 70, plan the colour placement for the windows, using several shades of fabric if desired. Cut the windows from the desired fabrics, using the window templates on pages 79–80. You will need Window Templates #1–#6, identified by number in the window plan.

6. Lay each cut window on the block to check that you like the effect. Stitch each window in place, matching the sewing thread to the background fabric.

Tip

The joined triangular shapes produce a double layer of folds that require careful handling while stitching but add an intriguing final effect.

KINGFISHER BLUE HANGING

Colour photo on page 82
Finished Quilt Size: 27½" x 27½"

Quilt Plan

☐ Fabric A   ▦ Fabric B   ▰ Fabric C

Window Plan

▨ Fabric 1   ░ Fabric 2   ☐ Fabric 3

▧ Fabric 4   ▰ Fabric 5

Materials

(44"-wide fabric)
½ yd. Fabric A for folded background shapes
¾ yd. Fabric B for folded background shapes
1 yd. Fabric C for folded background shapes
⅛ to ¼ yd. each of 5 different fabrics for windows
⅞ yd. for backing
⅞ yd. of 2-ounce polyester batting
¼ yd. for binding

Cutting and Block Construction

1. Referring to the quilt plan, cut the following pieces:
    Fabric A
        8 Right Triangle Template (page 78) for the triangular blocks
    Fabric B
        12 squares, each 8½" x 8½"
    Fabric C
        16 Rectangle Template 4 (page 58) for the rectangles
        4 squares, each 4½" x 4½"

2. Construct the Cathedral Window folded triangles from Fabric A, following the directions for "Making Folded Triangles" on page 66. Join them in pairs to make squares.

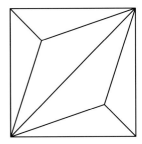

3. Construct Cathedral Window squares from Fabric B and Fabric C, following the directions beginning on page 10.
4. Construct the folded rectangles from Fabric C, following the directions beginning on page 41.

Quilt Top Assembly and Finishing

1. Following the quilt plan on page 72, join the folded squares and rectangles into rows, then stitch the rows together to form the final design, matching seams carefully. You may prefer to join the center block of squares first and then work outwards, adding the windows as you go.
2. Make templates for the windows by tracing the 7 shapes on pages 79–80.
3. Following the window plan for window location (numbers) and colour placement (shading), cut the following pieces from the desired fabrics, pinning them in place temporarily on the prepared background:

Window Fabric #1: 4 Window Template #1*
Window Fabric #2: 4 Window Template #7*
*These two window shapes create the central star shape when stitched in place. If using silk, take care to keep the grain of the fabric on all the pieces in the same direction or the colour will not appear to be the same.
Window Fabric #3: 8 Window Template #2 and 4 Window Template #3
Window Fabric #4: 8 Window Template #3 and 8 Window Template #4
Window Fabric #5: 8 Window Template #4, 12 Window Template #5, and 8 Window Template #6

4. Working from the center out, pin and sew the windows in position.
5. Following the directions on page 97, measure, cut, back with batting, and add mitered borders to the quilt top. Cut border strips and batting strips 4½" wide.
6. Back the quilt and tie at regular intervals to hold the layers together, referring to the directions on page 99.
7. Quilt as desired or mark quilting lines from each seam junction out to the edge of the border, continuing the diagonal line from each folded block. Refer to the quilt photo on page 82.
8. Bind the edges.

CREAM TWISTED WINDOW CUSHION

Colour photo on page 84
Finished Cushion Size: 12" x 12"

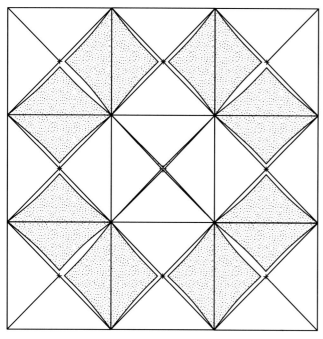

Cushion Plan

Completed Cushion

Materials

(44"-wide fabric)
¾ yd. cream-coloured cotton
Assorted light and dark pink scraps
2 yds. narrow cream-coloured lace edging
12"-square foam cushion or polyester fiberfill
for stuffing

Note

The center folded square is a combination of Cathedral Window and Secret Garden units.

To construct the center folded square:

1. Construct a folded Secret Garden square for the center, but instead of cutting the window to fit the folded square exactly, cut it ¼" larger all the way around.

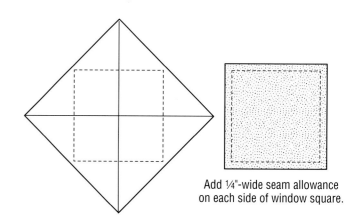

Add ¼"-wide seam allowance
on each side of window square.

2. Turn and press the ¼"-wide seam allowance to the wrong side of the window all around.

3. Appliqué the resulting square in place on the folded square.

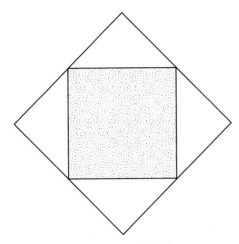

Appliqué square onto folded square.

4. Bring the 4 corners of the folded square to the center over the appliquéd square and bartack in place as usual. When the edges are rolled back and stitched to make a Cathedral Window, the underlayer of contrasting fabric adds extra colour.

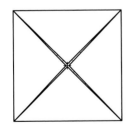

Folded square with extra layer
concealed at this stage

Cutting and Construction

1. From the cream-coloured cotton fabric, cut 9 squares, each 5" x 5".
2. Construct the central folded square with its Secret Garden insert as shown at left, using a 2¾" square of a dark pink fabric for the window.
3. Construct the remaining 8 folded squares, following the directions for steps 1 and 2 for "Constructing Twisted Windows" on pags 68–69.
4. Arrange the completed units in 3 rows of 3 each with the Secret Window square in the center. Join the squares into rows and then join the rows with whipstitching as usual, being careful to match the seams.
5. Remove the pins from the triangular shaded sections shown in the illustration below. Ignore the 16 flapping triangles and secure the remaining corners at the center of each folded square with a pair of tiny stitches through all layers as shown.

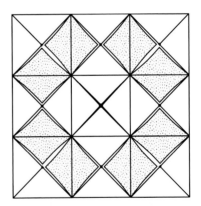

6. Fold the loose triangles as shown below and stitch each corner in place with 2 tiny stitches through all layers. Press carefully so that each folded spear shape is well defined.

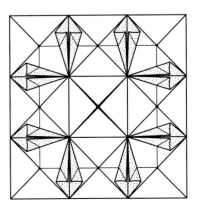

7. Cut 4 window squares, each 1½" x 1½", from a pink print. Position and stitch in place around the center Secret Garden window, following the directions on page 14 for adding windows to the classic Cathedral Window shape. When these are stitched in place, the darker pink fabric beneath is also revealed.

8. Cut 4 small squares of dark pink fabric, each measuring 1⅛" x 1⅛". Slip each piece between the layers of each corner folded square, using the points of a small pair of scissors to ensure the fabric is pushed right into the outside quarter section of the folded square. The shaded area in the illustration indicates the position under the layers of the folded background square.

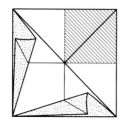

This square will be held in place when the folded edges are curved back and stitched so it will be quite secure. Again, it adds a little colour in the corners of the block.

9. Referring to the illustration above right, roll back the remaining folded edges, stitching with a small backstitch as for classic Cathedral Windows.

Stitch the 4 corner petal shapes as shown for Secret Garden units, using bartack stitches at each end to prevent the raw-edge corners of the underlying pink fabric from showing.

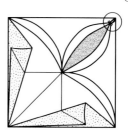

10. From the cream-coloured cotton, cut 2 squares, each 12½" x 12½". Set 1 square aside for the backing. On the remaining square, apply the narrow lace as shown, positioning it so the outer edges of the completed Twisted Window block just cover the inner straight edge of the lace. Miter the lace corners.

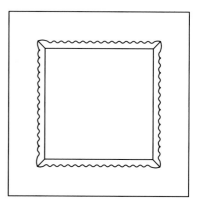

11. From a scrap of dark pink fabric, cut 8 squares, each 1¼" x 1¼" and 4 squares, each 2¼" x 2¼". From a scrap of light pink fabric, cut 12 squares, each 1¼" x 1¼".

12. Fold each square in half, wrong sides together, and press. Then bring the short ends of each rectangle to meet at the center and press to finish the folded triangles.

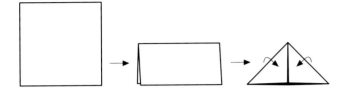

13. Arrange the folded triangles in 4 identical sets as shown; baste together across the raw edges.

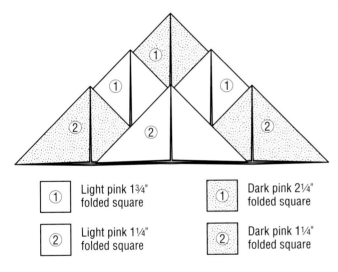

| ① | Light pink 1¾" folded square | ① | Dark pink 2¼" folded square |
| ② | Light pink 1¼" folded square | ② | Dark pink 1¼" folded square |

14. Center a cluster of folded triangles on each side of the lace square on the pillow top and baste in place. Then appliqué the completed Nine-Square block onto the cream square, covering the inner edge of the lace and the raw edges of the folded triangles. Position and stitch another band of lace 1½" from the outer edges of the block to complete the cushion top.

Finishing

1. With right sides together, stitch the cushion backing to the cushion front, using a ¼"-wide seam allowance and leaving an opening on one side for turning. Trim corners and turn the cushion right side out.

2. Insert the foam cushion or stuff the cushion cover with polyester fiberfill. Whipstitch the opening edges together.

3. Optional: Cover a small button with dark pink fabric and stitch it to the center of the finished cushion, drawing the stitches through all layers to pull the center of the cushion slightly inward for added dimension.

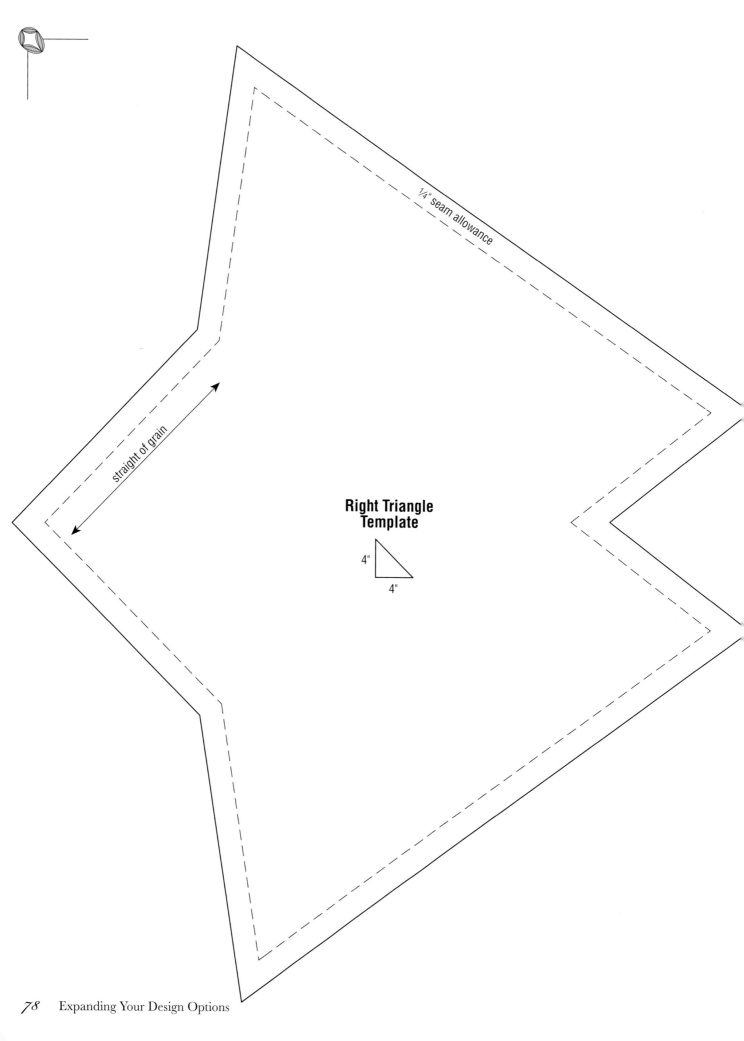

¼" seam allowance

straight of grain

**Right Triangle
Template**

4"

4"

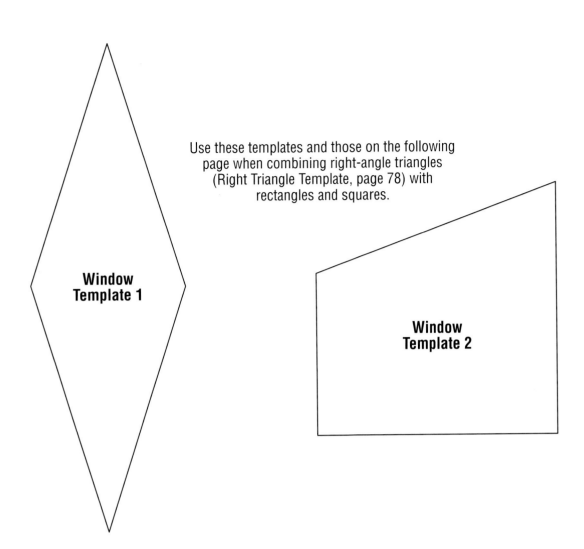

**Window
Template 1**

Use these templates and those on the following
page when combining right-angle triangles
(Right Triangle Template, page 78) with
rectangles and squares.

**Window
Template 2**

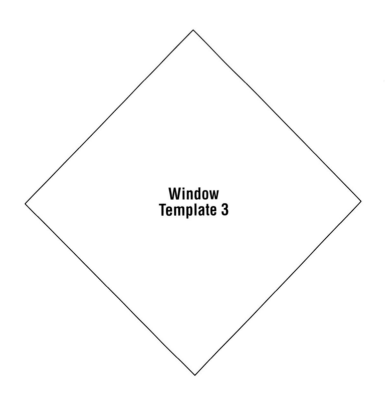

**Window
Template 3**

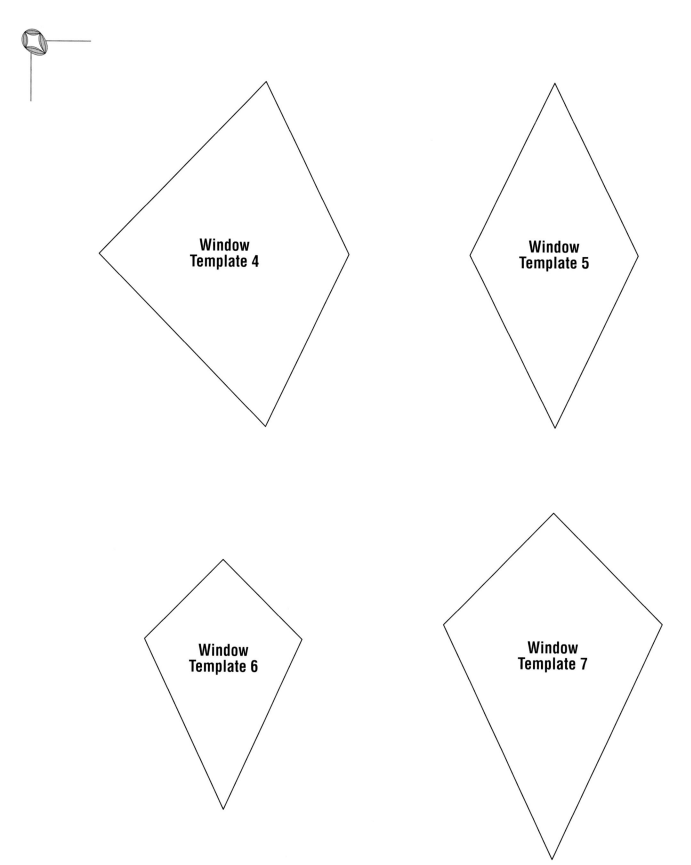

Window Template 4

Window Template 5

Window Template 6

Window Template 7

Nine-Block Quilt
by Lynne Edwards, 1991, Suffolk, England, 1991, 36" x 36".
In this quilt, I used nine repeats of the Nine Patch block shown on page 70. The folded background shapes were all cut from the same textured cotton fabric, but the silk windows vary in colour. Colour filters across each block, gradually deepening from the rows in the upper left corner to the lower right corner. Owned by Teressa Gordon-Jones.

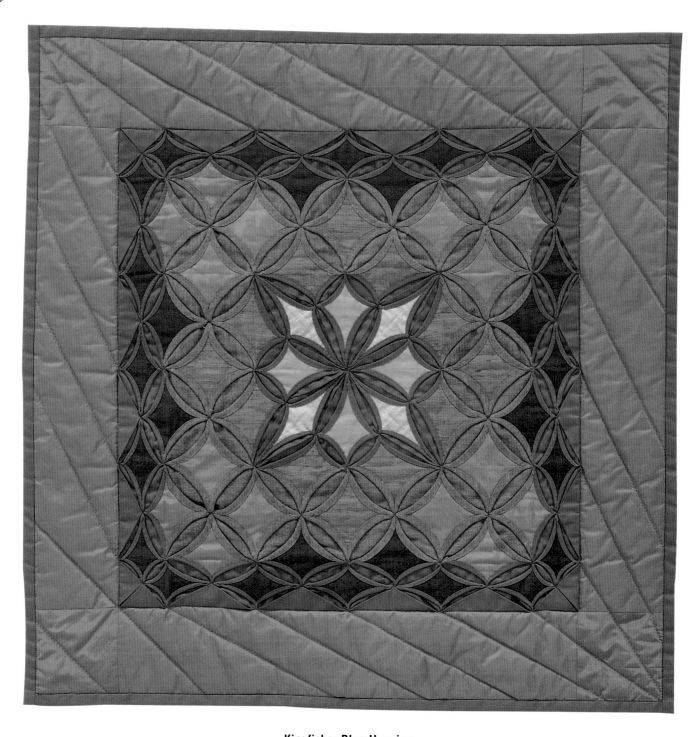

Kingfisher Blue Hanging
by Lynne Edwards, 1990, Suffolk, England, 27 1/2" x 27 1/2".
This quilt is made of four Nine Patch blocks arranged so that the triangular units meet in the center. Owned by Wendy Rulton.

Twisted Window Cushions
by Ann Larkin, 1992–1993, Suffolk, England, 15" x 15" and 12" x 12".
These beautiful cushions showcase exciting Twisted Window variations of the classic Cathedral Window.

Cream Cushion
by Ann Larkin, 1993, Suffolk, England, 12" x 12".
The design for this cushion is based on a nine-square design with a lace-edged frame.
The center folded square is a combination of Cathedral Window and Secret Garden units. Lace and prairie points are special embellishments.

Peacock Blues

by Maureen Baker, 1993, Essex, England, 32" x 32". This elegant piece was made of squares and rectangles with a center of glowing Cathedral Windows and Secret Garden squares in the four corners.

Bluebell Wood

by Audrey Benson, 1994, Sussex, England, 35" x 25½".

This design was derived from the accompanying preliminary sketch of a bluebell wood, using squares and rectangles.

Cathedral Window Cushion
by Hilda Bradbury, 1994, Shropshire, England. 7½" x 15".
Tiny Secret Garden squares decorate this ornate cushion.

Four Seasons
by Jean Constantine, 1994, Essex, England, 24" x 24".
This design features a chequerboard center of folded squares surrounded by rectangles and a larger Secret Garden square in each corner.

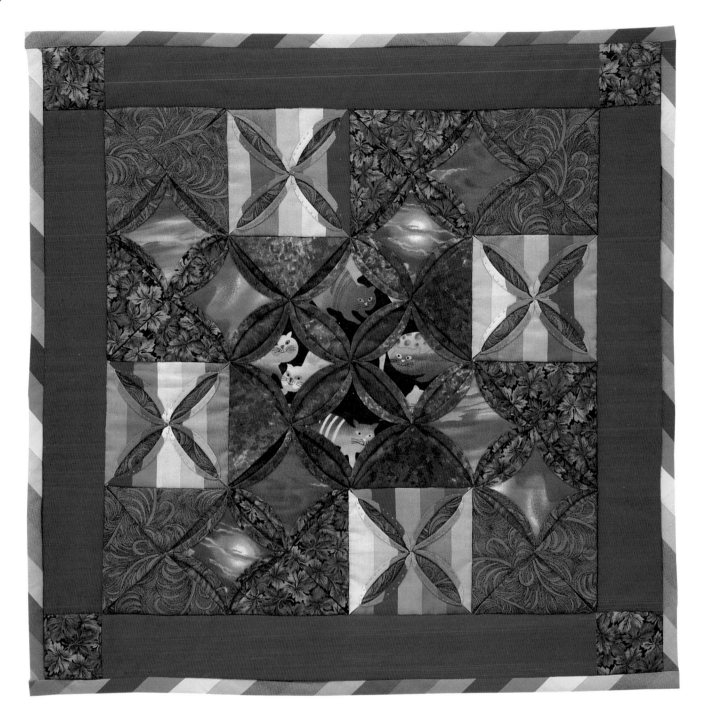

Cathedral Cats

by Jo Jeffries, 1994, Yorkshire, England, 19" x 19".
Jo made a simple block combining Classic Cathedral Window and Secret Garden squares in rather wild fabrics to create a stunning effect.

Thanksgiving for Autumn

by Elizabeth Snodgrass, 1994, Nottingham, England, 40" x 40".

Elizabeth used the classic Cathedral Window to create this piece inspired by the autumn colors in an English garden.

Just for Me
by Shirley Stocks, 1994, Suffolk, England, 26" x 29".
Satin windows in many tones glow in this combination of square and rectangular units.

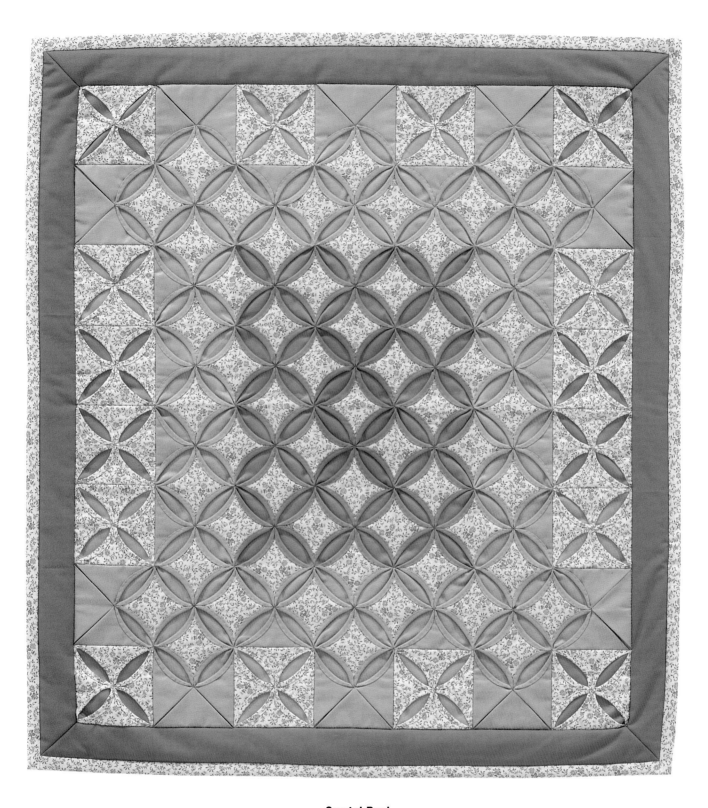

Crystal Pool
by Chris Wase, 1994, Suffolk, England, 28" x 31½".
In this design, Cathedral Window squares in the center reach out to the Secret Garden units in the corners and along the sides.

Secret Squares

by Sara Impey, 1992, Essex, England, 39" x 39".
Gradated tones of blue and pink are divided by a grid of black in this stunning quilt that showcases Sara's individual style in the
Secret Garden variation of Cathedral Window. She overdyes solid and patterned fabrics, and combines them with
solid black in her exciting designs. The Secret Garden windows also shift gradually from one shade to another.
The black corner areas are quilted in the same petal shape as the windows.

Secret Shades
by Sara Impey, 1993, Essex, England, 29" x 36".
In this chequerboard design, each coloured Secret Garden square alternates with a black Secret Garden square.
Colour shifts from one area to another through the patterned squares and in the windows.

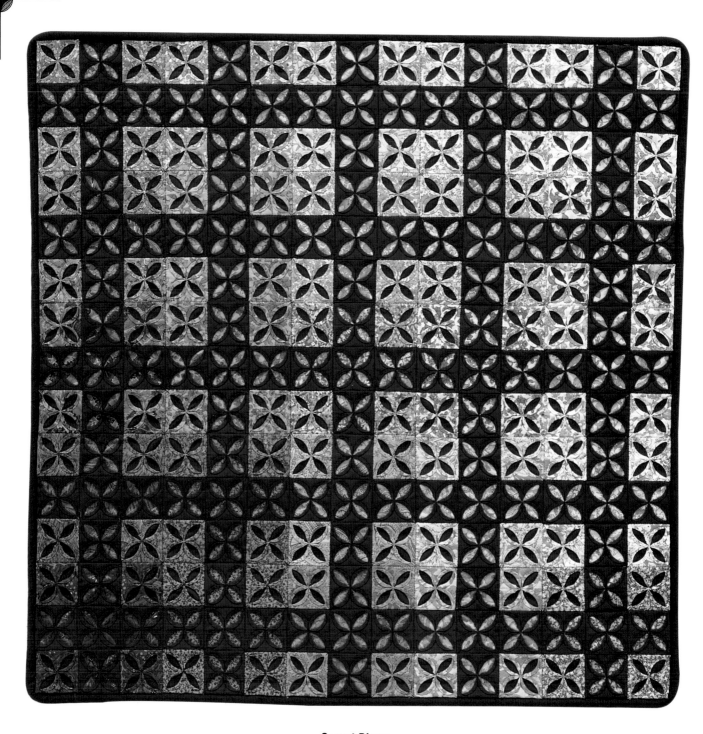

Secret Blues

by Sara Impey, 1993, Essex, England, 19½" x 19½".
Light travels from the top right to the bottom left in this small hanging, made of Secret Garden folded squares that measure only 1½" x 1½".
The black squares form a contrasting grid across which the color filters from light to dark.

Folded Windows

by Edna Farrow, 1992, Suffolk, England, 10" x 25 ½".

Windows of folded, hand-dyed fabrics were combined with squares and rectangles in this textured piece.

Finishing

Techniques

for

Cathedral

Window

Quilts

One of the bonuses of the Cathedral Window technique is that, once the folded squares are joined together, the quilt needs no further edging nor any backing for that matter. The thickness of the four layers of fabric adds weight and body and as long as the back looks tidy, the whole thing is finished once the last window is stitched and it can be put straight on the bed. A quilt made in this way should have stitches that are as inconspicuous and neat as possible. Small backstitches or knots buried in the layers begin and end the stitching as in quilting, so knots don't show on the back of the work. I always wish that I could find a way of leaving the backs of my quilts uncovered, as the mixture of colours and different shapes seen from the back makes another completely different quilt design.

If you want to be more creative and join Cathedral Window blocks into more complex projects, there are special challenges and considerations when it comes to adding sashing and borders. That is because the finished blocks do not have raw edges that can be stitched together in the conventional way.

I like to border the Cathedral Window center, as I find it tightens the design and adds a frame to the work. In the same way, repeated blocks need to be broken up with sashing as they can lose their impact without it. This is, of course, only my opinion on my own work; other quilters approach their designs differently and make their own decisions.

Because the borders and sashing strips need to be brought up to the same thickness as the folded blocks, I back them with lightweight batting. This then has to be covered on the reverse side, and the simplest way to do this is to back the entire quilt. I have found also that a Cathedral Window wall hanging needs the support of backing fabric to hold the weight in place and prevent sagging after hanging for a length of time.

Adding Sashing and Borders

Two quilt projects in the book have sashing—the "Knot Garden Quilt" shown on page 16 and the "Purple Quilt" shown on page 27. Detailed instructions for backing the sashing strips with batting appear in the directions for each of these. You can adapt these instructions to any of your own designs by altering the measurements according to the size of the quilt blocks.

I find it helpful to postpone the decision about borders until the quilt top is approaching completion. It is tempting to plan the whole thing as you begin, especially when you're calculating fabric quantities, but it is only when the quilt is finally together that you can really decide on the best frame for your design.

As you select possible fabrics for the border, try pinning a strip around the quilt to get the effect and to make the final decision on the width of the border. As with sashing strips, border strips also need a thin layer of batting so the border strips have a weight and body similar to the Cathedral Window units that make up the center of the quilt top. I prefer to add borders with mitered corners.

Adding a Mitered Border

1. Determine how wide you will need to cut the border strips by first deciding how wide you wish the finished border to be. Remember that the outer edge of the border will be bound, so take that into account in your calculations. Add a ¼"-wide seam allowance to the desired finished border width.

2. Measure the quilt through the center in both the lengthwise and crosswise directions and record these measurements. Do not measure the outer edges. The most stretch in a quilt top happens along the outer edges. Cutting strips to match the quilt measurements through the center helps ensure that the finished quilt is square and straight.

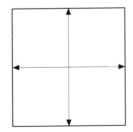

3. To the measurements determined in step 2, add ½" plus 2 times the border-strip width determined in step 1. For example, if the quilt

length is 60" and you want to cut 5"-wide border strips (including seam allowances), add 10½" and cut 2 strips, each 5" x 70½". Many quiltmakers prefer to add a little more than the extra ½" for seam allowances, just to be safe, and trim away the excess after stitching the mitered corners.

4. Repeat step 3 for the crosswise dimension of the quilt and cut 2 border strips of the determined length for the top and bottom borders.

5. Mark the quilt measurement at each end of each border strip with a pin, or use a marking pencil.

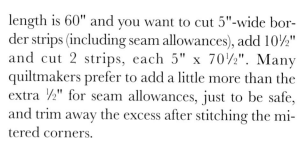

6. Back each strip with a piece of 2-ounce batting and machine stitch through both layers ¼" away from the marked edge.

7. Trim the batting close to the stitching.

8. Using a sharp marking pencil, draw a line 45° from the marked points at the stitching line out to the other long edge on each of the 4 border strips. I use the 45° line on my Rotary Rule to do this. Keep the drawn line as light as possible. It's just a guide for stitching. Machine stitch through the strips and batting along the lines.

9. On each border strip, fold the seam allowance over the batting so the machine stitches lie along the fold.

10. Pin the strip to the edge of the Cathedral Window quilt top, right sides together, matching the marked points on the strip to the corners of the quilt. You may well have to ease in some full-

ness in the Cathedral Window edges to fit the border strip. Distribute any fullness evenly and pin along the length. Whipstitch together in the same way you sew Cathedral Window squares together to make the quilt top.

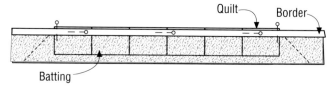

11. After attaching all border strips to the quilt in the manner shown, miter the corners. Fold the quilt diagonally with right sides together at one corner so that the two border strips are lying on top of each other.

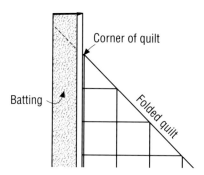

12. Pushing the seam allowance toward the quilt, position the two machine-stitched lines on top of each other and pin. Stitch along these lines through both layers of border fabric and batting, either by hand or by machine.

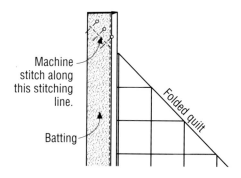

Open out the mitered corner and check to see whether any of the original machine stitching is visible from the front. If it is, either remove it or stitch once more just inside the first row of stitching. Trim the batting as close to the stitching as possible. Trim the excess fabric down to a ¼"-wide seam allowance and finger-press it open. Light pressing is possible on the right side of the border with a cool iron, taking care not to let the iron come into contact with the batting. Repeat this process on all four corners of the quilt.

Backing and Tying

1. To back the quilt, cut a piece of fabric that measures approximately ½" larger than the quilt itself on all sides. Place the backing fabric right side down on a flat surface with the quilt centered on it right side up. Since the Cathedral Window top needs to be held in place on the backing and as it is too thick to quilt comfortably, tying is the best solution. Pin at regular intervals (about 4" apart) and at junctions of the blocks to mark the places for tying.

2. To tie, thread a needle with a length of cotton thread (not quilting thread, which is too springy for tight knots) in a colour that matches the quilt. Use it doubled but do not knot the ends. Bring the needle up from the back through all layers and return it to the back, making a small stitch in the front that hopefully will not be noticeable. Remove the marker pin and turn the quilt to the back. Cut the threads so that both double ends measure about 2" to 3". Tie these in a knot, tying first right over left and then left over right. Tie again in the same manner for a secure knot. Repeat at each marked position for the ties. Trim the thread ends to ¼" to ½" after knotting.

Quilting

The border may be quilted or left plain. I like to stitch in-the-ditch along the seam lines, joining the border to the quilt top, as this helps hold the quilt top in place on the backing. This is particularly helpful if the project is a wall hanging, which may be heavy and might sag without this extra stitching. Additional quilting is not necessary, but you may wish to add it for decorative reasons. Many of the quilts shown in this book have been quilted as well as tied.

Binding

After attaching borders, adding the backing, and quilting, it's time to bind the edges.

1. Trim any excess batting and backing fabric even with the outer edges of the border.
2. Cut binding strips 2" wide to bind the edges. Cut 2 strips that match the length of the quilt top and 2 strips that are each 1½" longer than the top and bottom edges of the quilt. The resulting binding will be ½" wide.
3. Fold each strip in half lengthwise with wrong sides together. Open each pressed strip and bring in the raw edges to the center crease. Press. Then fold in half again and press.

4. Open a binding strip for one long edge of the quilt and pin to the quilt, with the raw edge of the binding extending above the raw edge of the quilt very slightly. This helps accommodate the thickness of the batting when you fold it over the edge of the quilt.
5. If you have a walking foot or an even-feed feature on your machine, now is the time to use it

as you stitch the binding to the quilt top. It helps keep the layers from creeping and shifting as you stitch. Stitch ½" from the edge of the binding in the crease line.

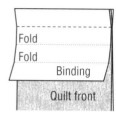

6. Fold the binding over the raw edge and slipstitch the folded edge in place along the stitching line. If necessary, trim the ends of the binding to match the quilt edges. Repeat on the remaining long edge of the quilt.

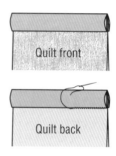

7. Machine stitch the binding to the top and bottom edges of the quilt in the same manner, leaving about ¾" of the binding extending at each end. After stitching, trim excess, leaving at least ½" at each end to fold in over the quilt before turning the binding to the back and slipstitching in place.

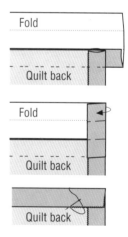

Meet the Author

English quilter Lynne Edwards has been making quilts since the early 1970s. After making her first Cathedral Window quilt in 1977, she was hooked on the design. It wasn't until five years later, when she saw a traditional Cathedral Window quilt, that she realized she was supposed to use muslin and scraps. By then, it was too late, and the heady game of designing with color and different shapes had taken over. Along with developing her Cathedral Window technique, for which she is probably best known, Lynne writes, teaches, and lectures on other quiltmaking techniques, including machine quilting, on which she has produced a video. Lynne and her husband live in a sixteenth-century house in a village in Suffolk, England.